FORBIDDEN VOICE

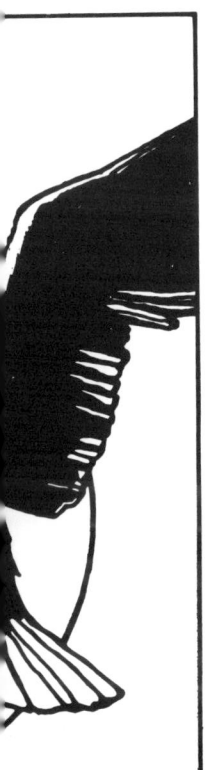

Alma Greene
(Gah-wonh-nos-doh)

FORBIDDEN VOICE

Reflections of a
Mohawk
Indian

Illustrations
and Cover Design by
Gordon McLean

GREEN DRAGON PRESS
TORONTO CANADA

First published in 1972 by
The Hamlyn Publishing Group
London New York Sydney Toronto

Re-issued 1997 by

Green Dragon Press
135 George Street South, #902
Toronto, ON M5A 4E8

Canadian Cataloguing in Publication Data

Greene, Alma, 1896-1983
    Forbidden voice : reflections of a Mohawk Indian

ISBN 1-896781-04-7

1. Greene, Alma, 1896-1983. 2. Mohawk Indians.
3. Mohawk Indians - Ontario - Biography. I. Title.

E99.M8G733 1997   970'.0049755   C97-930205-6

FOREWORD

I am very proud to be Alma Green's grand-daughter. She left us all such a wonderful legacy in her book, *Forbidden Voice: Reflections of a Mohawk Indian*. All her life she tried to encourage a deeper understanding of the Native community by the non-native community, and when *Forbidden Voice* was first published, it showed so many people that we are a proud, culturally rich nation, with traditions and beliefs worthy of respect.

It is important for new generations, both non-native and Native, to continue this learning process. *Forbidden Voice* is an invaluable resource for the education of other cultures about our way of life, and for the preservation of our culture.

Lori M. Greene

My mother would have been proud for her book to be reprinted. It is very much in demand and mom's intention when she wrote the book was to show non-native people our way of life, so they would have a better understanding of our people. She would be happy so many people are interested in her work.

Marie H. Greene

Mom was always trying to bridge the gap between the Native and the non-native people. She wanted our traditions and culture to be kept alive and known, so that others would understand what it was like growing up as a Mohawk Clan Mother. She told her stories about our traditions and beliefs so they would be preserved and passed on from generation to generation among her own people. In this way, these traditions and her life would live on forever.

Jeannette Y. Greene

CONTENTS

A YOUNG PRINCESS

Childhood in the Grand River Lands

As a small native girl of the Six Nations, Forbidden Voice was a princess of royal blood, heiress to her mother, who was a clan mother to a chieftainship title.

In the beginning the Great Spirit had formed the Iroquois League of Peace and ordained good men of each tribe who became lords of the Confederacy Fire, and their title was to be passed down, tracing descent of blood through the female line, and was to live forever. Her mother, who was a Mohawk of the Turtle Clan, belonged to one of these hereditary lines. The female beings were very important in the confederacy for they could decide which male in each eternal clan was fit to inherit the chieftainship, and could even depose a chief; they had other powers as well. The oldest brother in a family, if he were judged fit, would inherit the title of ordained chief through the mother, and in time the little native girl herself might become a clan mother.

The little girl's father was also a Mohawk of the Wolf Clan, for a clan mother has a sacred duty to marry within her tribe and must not marry a man of a different clan. He must be either a bear, a wolf or a turtle–these are the clans of the Mohawk Tribe.

Her father was a good man, he gave up his time for the good of the council fire, he could act as interpreter and secretary and many times represented the Confederacy Council as one of a delegation on an important mission. The chiefs of the confederacy appreciated his work and made him a Pine Tree Chief, for the Great Spirit had given them the right to better their government.

The small girl lived with her mother and father, two grown-up brothers and an older sister, on a farm of fifty acres, just inside the edge of the Grand River Lands. This was a part of the land grant of 1784–six miles wide on each side of the Grand River–to the Six Nations Indians for remaining loyal to England in her war with the American Colonies.

The town of Brantford, Ontario, was quite nearby, but though more than half of the re-

serve was cleared and under cultivation, the rest was a wonderful place of moors, fens, marshes and bush with the beautiful Grand River flowing through. Birds and wild game were everywhere.

The place where they lived was a large frame house set among huge stately trees—maples, oaks, elms, birch, walnut, hickory, basswood and black ash—and at the back was a pond where the little girl fished in the summer and skated in the winter. In the fields there were corn, oats, barley, wheat, potatoes, turnips, pumpkins, carrots and radishes.

In the farmyard there were pigs, chickens, turkeys, ducks, geese, calves and twenty-six milking cows—in the pasture were four work horses and a race horse, a beautiful grey mare and her baby colt.

Inside the house there was a parlour with a red carpet padded underneath with straw, on the walls were bright colored paper, a large red-glass parlour lamp, an old fall-leaf table with a red paisley table cloth. On the table were knick-knacks, a century old—a milk glass hen on a nest and in the nest were three blue eggs.

In the dining room was a long table and chairs, an old fashioned wood heater and a huge secretary which reached the ceiling; the floor was painted a light green and there were braided scatter mats in various colors.

In the kitchen was an old fashioned cook stove, behind it was a large pantry for baking and washing dishes, next to it was a wash room, where you could wash your face and take a bath in privacy. Underneath the kitchen was a large, cool cellar; at one end the milk was stored and cream ready to be churned into butter, and at the other end hogs were dressed and cured for winter meat.

Upstairs were three large bedrooms; the little native girl slept in a room with her mother. It had two beds, two windows and a heating pipe from the stove below.

It was a happy and exciting life for a little girl. In the fruit season she would go with the women of the neighborhood to pick wild

berries for winter food or to take to the Trading Post, which was in the Market Square at Brantford. The women went together to the big woods, for there were rattlesnakes and it was quite dangerous. Before they went, everybody rubbed lard on their shoes – the pig is the enemy of the snake, and because lard is condensed from pork, the rattlesnake has a keen sense of his enemy and keeps his distance.

In the fall the women gathered the pumpkins from the fields; they sliced and cut them in strips and hung the half circles on a long pole over the stove to dry, then they could cook the pumpkin as a vegetable in the winter or have pumpkin pies.

They also brought in the white field beans on their vine, and neighbors came at night to help thresh and clean the beans for winter's food.

Best of all there was always a barrel of molasses which they bought from the flour mills in Brantford, this was used like the syrup of today; it was so delicious to come in from the cold to a treat of hot biscuits and molasses.

Every Friday night the little girl helped her mother to get ready for market, early next morning. First the mother would cut the heads off a dozen chickens, then the family worked together to pluck the feathers and carefully take out all the pin feathers.

Next came the butter printing; the butter was put into a mould which held exactly a pound and had a beautiful rose design in the centre. The little girl would go outside with a lantern and pick the biggest rhubarb leaves. These would be plunged into a bucket of ice cold water, shaken out and used to wrap up the butter overnight to keep it cold and firm.

In the morning everybody got up before sunrise, eggs were gathered from the barn and each one washed by hand, these too were going to the market. The little girl got more fresh rhubarb leaves and re-wrapped the butter. All was now ready. Then the father hitched up the horses to the democrat and was off for the market. The mother would use the money from the sale of fresh eggs, butter and chickens to buy groceries and clothing for her family.

The little girl herself was never taken into Brantford except when she needed new shoes. When she did go, the greatest attraction was a life-size bear standing upright outside one of the shops. At lunch time her father would sit on the edge of the board sidewalk where the other Indian families all sat to eat their lunches. The little girl never had anything to do with white children at all. She was not allowed to and neither did she want to. Even at that time she realized that she was different from them and they often made fun of her; she knew that her creator was in the wind, in the sunshine and in the silence of the night.

At home she tried to do everything her two brothers did, she pitched horseshoes with them in the summer and in the winter joined with them in throwing snowsnakes. Snowsnakes were made out of slender pieces of hickory about six feet long, carved in the form of a snake. Her brothers made them and took great pride in carving them to look lifelike, with lead set in to make the mouth; they also made special wax polish for them to suit every kind of snow, wet or dry. They made a track by dragging a straight log through the snow, and if the weather was zero, they would pour water on the track to make it icy. The game was to see which snake would go farthest, and spectators would place small bets on the snake of their choice. The tail was notched to make a finger grip, and you ran to get momentum and threw the snake underhand. On moonlight nights the little girl loved to watch the snowsnakes glisten as they sped along the track.

Her two brothers made their own bows and arrows to go hunting with, so she made her own and never missed a target; later on she learned to handle a rifle like any man. Her brothers were grown men, her sister was also much older and she had friends her own age. The little girl was left alone a lot, but she found great happiness in living in her own make-believe world.

She went down to the pond and the ducks came out of the water to race for pieces of bread she threw them. She caught polywogs in the pond and watched the frogs catch flies; she watched the squirrels in the trees, and it was not long before she could climb as well as they did.

In the fall when her father was cutting the hay and oats, she followed behind him looking for the mouse nests he uncovered; she would pick out the live baby mice and fill her pockets with them to take home for the cats.

There were also two dogs, called Tori and Jack who were her constant companions. They killed all the snakes that came into the garden and loved to play tug-of-war with one of their victims. Every day she would make lunch and go into the bush at the back of the house with Tori and Jack; there she talked to all the living things in her native Mohawk, for she spoke no English.

Nature taught her many things – for example she could tell when a storm was coming, the leaves from the shrubs and trees would turn over and show their silvery undersides. The pigs in the barnyard would run back and forth carrying leaves and twigs in their mouths to build a fort against the oncoming storm and the robin high in the tree would call out 'yo-ronh-yo-ronh, yo-ronh-yo-ronh', which meant, 'it is cloudy, it is going to rain'.

Once when the little girl was eleven she became ill with a fever. In the middle of it her mother took her out of bed, bundled her up and drove into town to have her picture taken. This was in case the little girl got worse and died – there would be some record of her for her mother who had had much sorrow. She had given birth to nine children and had only four left – three precious babies had died in their infancy and later on a daughter who was sixteen years old. The mother had her fortune read and was told that she would lose all her children if she continued to doubt her belief, her own birth-given right belief, the belief of her forefathers.

Her husband, Forbidden Voice's father, who had elaborated in the white trailing gown of the select, was shocked and broken-hearted when he was called to his dying girl's bedside. She covered her face with her frail and almost transparent hands and told him to go quickly and take the reindeer out of his nose. He quickly left the room and got on his knees to pray and when he arose and went back into her bedroom, she smiled so sweetly and told him he had it all fixed up. She passed away in the early hours of a new dawn with a smile on her face – she was only sixteen.

Forbidden Voice's father had followed Joseph Brant in his new religion of the Anglican denomination and donned the white trailing robes of the priests and took a prominent part in the affairs of the church. He had confused the mind of his daughter, Josephine, on her dying bed.

This had happened before Forbidden Voice was born. When she was fourteen years old, she became the organist of the church.

One Sunday morning as she played the closing hymn of the service, she heard another choir which seemed to come from an open window. When she played the second verse, the choir from the outside sang loud and clear; it was not the same hymn she was playing, they were singing 'O Jesu I Have Promised'.

She stopped playing. The minister and her father went quickly to her side and carried her out of the church. For many days she thought about what had happened, and wondered if it was a revelation of a promise she had once given and broken; had she betrayed the faith of her forefathers?

Forbidden Voice is an old lady now, and this book shall reveal the things she has seen and heard which have never been told before.

THE PRINCESS AND THE DEER

The gift of healing
Nature's medicines
Prophecies and omens

The little girl's proper memory was of being weaned when she was four years old. One day her mother decided it was time, painted one of her breasts red to resemble blood, bandaged it and sat huddled in her rocking chair as if in great pain.

Early that morning, neighbors had come to help her father kill pigs for the coming winter's food. At this time there is always a great commotion, pigs squealing and men running back and forth, so Forbidden Voice decided to go back to the house. When she found her mother in great pain, she came to her own conclusion—that a pig had bitten her mother. That night she slept in the room with her father; the next day she took a nursing bottle full of milk to school with her. In mid-morning the teacher called Forbidden Voice and set her under his desk and gave her the bottle to nurse. The teacher was Indian; the reserve schools never kept a white teacher for long.

For Forbidden Voice was still nursing at the breast when she first saw the little deer. One day she wandered into the bush at the back of the house, with Tori and Jack, and she must have lain down in the shade on the soft ground and fallen asleep. They must have missed her at the farmhouse, for she was awakened by a tall lady in a red apron, someone she knew, though not by name, who had been looking for her. When the lady picked her up, Forbidden Voice saw a fawn standing with the dogs where she had just been sleeping. The fawn was no bigger than the dogs, not even a foot high. The tall lady said she didn't see him.

Every time Forbidden Voice went to that place in the bush the tiny deer was waiting for her. It would come out from under the May apple, which was a big plant, about eighteen inches high, with an umbrella of coarse, hairy leaves shaped like big oak leaves. It had fruit the size of walnuts that were poisonous if you ate them green; but if you buried them to turn yellow in the ground, they were supposed to be all right. The fawn would frisk over plants and nibble on the tender shoots of the wild raspberry and follow Forbidden Voice wherever she went, though it would never come out of the bush. It ate what she ate, and her mother got used to her carrying table scraps off to the woods to feed the fawn. Except for that first day with the tall lady, Forbidden Voice never saw the deer when anyone else was around.

She told her mother about her adventures with the deer, and by and by her mother got worried and consulted an old Indian chief. He told her not to interfere, for the little girl had been favored and blessed. The tiny deer, which few people have ever seen, was actually a sign that the time would come when she would help her people in sickness and give counsel in their distress.

Later on Forbidden Voice had a playmate her own age, whose father was a medicine man and owned a crystal ball which had been in his family for years. A long time ago, when his great, great grandfather was out hunting in a large forest along the Ohio Valley, he came upon an old man sitting on a log, who said he had something to give him. It was the crystal ball. He had got it from the mountain top where the little people, called fairies, played on moonlit nights. The old man told him what it was for and how to use it—the crystal ball was never intended for evil purposes but to help people—and when he became old, he should hand it down to the next of kin. Forbidden Voice and her friend had many discussions about it, and Forbidden Voice knew that she also had been born with a gift and that the gift had something to do with what the red man called medicine. The old people of her time told her all about Indian remedies and how to prepare them.

Remedies

The wild strawberry has great medicinal value. It is regarded as a sacred plant growing along the heaven-road. It is used for internal disorders and heart ailments.

The young shoots and tender leaves of the wild raspberry are used to enrich the blood. Make tea of the mixture and drink it lukewarm.

Mullen leaves picked and dried will relieve asthma and sore throat if smoked and inhaled through a new clay pipe. Mullen leaves are

usually found on pasture land.

Goose oil and skunk oil are used as a chest-rub for a cold. Warm the oil.

Adam leaves, crushed, pulverized and mixed with goose oil make an excellent healing ointment.

Forget-me-not is an important remedy to the red men. It is used to cure diarrhea, and in the treatment of cancer, and for birth control.

Foxglove is used for heart ailment and has been known to cure.

The fruit of the May apple, if buried till it turns yellow, will cure tuberculosis.

The roots of the wild apple tree facing eastward purify the kidneys and prevent the aches and pains of rheumatism. The apple roots are cut with an axe into chips. Fill a large kettle and boil the chips hard for two hours. Let the brew cool down and then drink often. Take from one to two gallons a day until relieved and well.

Tap the vine of a wild grape in the spring. Catch all the liquid you can and use it for your hair. It is excellent for baldness.

Get oil out of chicken fat, put it into a bottle. Used lukewarm, one drop in each ear, it will relieve deafness and sometimes cure. Use it twice a week at bedtime and always warm the oil.

Scrape downwards the twigs of elderberry bushes and fill two bags about eight inches square. Sew the openings tight, and put the bags in a steamer to steam. Place one bag over a swelling and keep changing it with the other until the swelling is better. This treatment is also beneficial for neuralgia.

Get up early on Good Friday. Do not talk to anyone. Take a glass jar and find a stream of running water. Facing the sun, dip your jar and fill it with the holy water and ask your Creator to bless this water. You will have a cure for every ill if you have faith.

All these remedies except for the last one are the herbal part of what the red men called medicine. The last remedy was *real* medicine, and so was the sacred tobacco.

The sacred tobacco was ordinary tobacco

that grew on the reserve, collected and dried but not cured. It had to be collected in a certain way, and not everyone could do the collecting—just certain people. They were called medicine men or medicine women. They couldn't talk about the ceremony of gathering the tobacco.

Burning it was a protection and a remedy and a prayer to the Creator. Nothing important was ever done without first burning the sacred tobacco. Whenever an Indian heard a rumble of distant thunder, for example, he would burn the sacred tobacco in thanksgiving for all things created, and to beseech most solemnly the protection of all mankind. Whenever there was sickness or trouble in a family, the sacred tobacco was burned. At every feast and cere-monial, every time a house was attacked by witchcraft, whenever anyone was worried or needed a counter-charm or wanted his prayers to work—the tobacco was burned. The Creator had given his people a promise that whenever they burned the sacred tobacco he would hearken to them.

Burning it was always a ceremony, and even the leavings were used, for they could be scattered at the door to give protection to the house.

Being the medicine man for a tribe was a very important thing. He was also the person who collected the roots and herbs for remedies. When the medicine man found the herb he required, he built a small fire beside it and threw sacred tobacco on the dying embers. As the smoke rose to the heavens, it blended with his humble supplications for the Great Spirit to grant mercy and to speak to the spirit of the herb to cast up its healing powers. The roots and herbs were gathered only at a certain time of the year. They were never picked during the season of the firebugs, for that is the season of witches, who also cause mysterious lights.

The medicine men and the witches had the same sort of powers, except that the medicine men used their powers for others' good and the witches for their own. Some witches are very evil and have given their souls to the devil in exchange for their powers.

Forbidden Voice felt rather special and queer about the divine gift for medicine that the old chief said she had. She had already seen the deer and knew she had another kind of gift that also made her feel strange.

Her mother was teaching her household tasks, and one of them was to gather the dishes after meals. She would peer into the teacups and read the formations in the tea leaves. She did not want to do this but her eyes were drawn to the cups and she could not resist.

One night when a chief and his wife had come for a meal, Forbidden Voice carried the chief's cup to the kitchen and saw in it horses running away and an upset buggy. She told her mother this, but her mother gave her a spank and sent her outside. After several days the chief went into town with a load of eggs, and his horses ran away and his buggy and eggs were smashed.

After that many things happened that she had seen beforehand in the cups. The little girl's mother, who had been brought up at Smoky Hollow among the whites, believed that people weren't supposed to know into the future, and scolded her, and told her she was wicked. Forbidden Voice was frightened and stopped telling what she could see, but she didn't stop seeing.

Because of the things she had told that had come true, people at parties joked with her about getting their cups read. But it wasn't a game with her, and she wondered if they knew the terrible feeling that came over her, guilt and fascination, when her eyes went to the tea leaves.

She never tried to tell her own fortune, but once, when she was seven she sent away for a reading of her life. This said she would die by drowning, and ever after that she was afraid of the water and did not like to go near the river.

It wasn't unusual for Indians to tell fortunes with tea leaves. But certain ones among them told fortunes with roots. All the Indians believed in omens and prophecies and had a great stock of them that had to do with what

fate had in store for the red men. When the time came for her to get her real name – her Indian name, not her name in white man's law – the name chosen for her was Gah-wonh-nos-doh. It meant Forbidden Voice.

Omens and Prophecies

When squirrels gather nuts abundantly in the fall of the year and fill their nests with food, I do likewise. The winter will be long and severe.

If the husks of corn are thick and heavy it will be a long, cold winter.

If a mother dreams she is gathering eggs, there is going to be an increase in her family.

If a mother does not want to lose her newborn baby, she will prepare a narrow thread of deerhide, and as soon as the baby has its first bath, she will tie the strip around its left wrist. There is a belief that a newborn child can still converse with the angels and if the newborn is not wanted on earth the angels will take it back. So if the baby should be asked to go home to heaven, the baby can say, 'I cannot go. I am tied up with my mother's love.'

If by accident a cloth is hung at the front door, someone may die. Black clothes are unlucky and are worn only for mourning.

If an owl screeches by your house three nights in a row, it is a bad omen. Someone will die.

If ants build an anthill close to your front door, you are being warned that a witch is pointing a finger at you and you are the next victim.

If you have lost an object of great value, you can find it by sleeping upon the ground alone, with a handful of grave dirt you have got from the cemetery. Hold it in your left hand, placing your hand under your head. A dead person will appear to you in a dream and reveal the mystery of the lost object. If you want to be led to your lost object, repeat this three nights in a row.

Take special heed at harvest time. If the corn you planted is barely three feet high and the cobs only three or four inches long, gather

27

your harvest and store it, for the last famine is at hand and the end of time is here.

If at any time the constitution of the Six Nations Confederacy, given by the Great Spirit, is violated or destroyed, the violators will take a few steps and will vomit blood, and tragedy and disaster will fall upon them.

It is predicted that sorrow and discontent shall enter the council chamber of the Six Nations Confederacy. But this dark cloud will pass and the Law of the Tree of Peace shall live forever.

It is predicted that when the red man is left between two fences, when the white man has crowded him so he has no more homes, then will the Great Spirit come again. The red man will gather a bushel of sacred tobacco, and burn it, and when the tobacco is all consumed, then will the Great Spirit, whose name is Dehganawihdeh, come.

There is a dream of a chief which is accepted as a prophecy. It was a long time before the white man discovered America, and this was the dream of an Indian chief of the Iroquois and he called his people together to tell them of it because he felt it had meaning. This was after the Great Spirit had established the League of Peace but before any Indian had seen a white man. In the chief's dream he had to leave home to deliver a message of great importance to another tribe whose settlement was many miles away. He left just before the break of day riding his favorite pony, and after he had travelled many miles he began to hear strange voices.

There was no one about the road which was deserted, but still he heard the voices. It was then he noticed that his pony had two heads instead of one. One head was that of a red man, wearing ceremonial headdress. The other head was also a human head, but it had fair skin and long curly blonde hair with a blonde moustache. The blond head spoke with a foreign tongue, but in his dream the chief could understand all the conversation. The blond head warned that there would be more and more blond heads until there would be no more room for the red men. He said his people

had no alternative, because where they lived now was so crowded that it was like a dark dungeon with snakes crawling in dark corners. The red man's head answered that his tribe had accepted Dehganawihdeh's message of peace and good will so the blonde head would be welcome. The blond head nodded his approval. Then the blond head stretched his neck and wound it round the red man's head and slowly strangled him to death.

The chief woke from this dream, but soon he fell asleep again and his dream continued. It seemed that the Indian tribes had been joined by strange people who spoke a strange language. The tribes held a council fire and instructed their chief warrior to go to the home of the four winds who travel the earth. No one can invade the home of the four winds unless the lives of man-beings are in danger. When the chief warrior reached his destination he was welcomed, and placed upon the cloud that is the honor seat for visitors, and then he told the four winds of the red man's trouble.

The four winds summoned the elements for a consultation, and asked each one to state his intentions for the man-beings.

First the four winds themselves spoke. They said their purpose was to enfold the man-beings and protect them from all harm, for the man-beings had accepted the message of peace and goodwill to all mankind. That is why the four winds had not slain the messenger.

Then the four winds said that the invaders with the strange tongue would stay only a little while, and when the time had ripened the winds would return them whence they had come. They spoke to the chief: 'Hold fast to your belief in peace. You are, like us, one of the created.'

Next the sun said, 'I give light and heat so that all things created may thrive and live.'

Then the moon said, 'I give light in the darkness and I govern the births of the man-beings. I too am one of the created.'

The thunder said, 'I am the grandfather of the man-beings. My first duty is to purify the earth. My second duty is to destroy the great serpents and reptiles on earth and in the sea.'

The sea said, 'I am the mother of the man-eings. All things are provided. The buffalo, ntelope, beaver and bear are their meat, and ive skins to keep them warm. The roots and erbs from my soil, and the fish from my treams, are sustenance for all.'

So all the elements of the universe assured ne chief warrior that everything was created or a purpose. They directed him to return to is tribe and tell them to hold fast to their faith and all would be well with them and they who accepted the message of peace, goodwill to all mankind shall see the heaven-road which leads to the home of the Blessed. The little girl knew so many stories of the heaven-world, she longed to be there. She knew that all things come from the Creator and she could hear His voice in the wind, thunder, rain and sunshine. He was everywhere.

MYTHS AND LEGENDS

Forbidden Voice was allowed to stay in the room when other men from the tribe came to visit her father, though this was not usual for children – particularly girl-children. The men came mostly on winter evenings, around nine-o'clock, for on a farm you work late, especially if you have livestock to feed. The wood fire in the old kitchen stove would already be dying. The men would come stamping in out of the cold, carrying kerosene lanterns which they turned down low and left in the kitchen, and then they would all go into the dining room to sit around the heater.

Sometimes the little girl passed apples for them to eat as they talked, and sometimes she fished into the barrel of broken crackers for the biggest pieces and toasted them on the back of the heater. But mostly she sat big-eyed at her oldest brother's feet or else perched on the long dining room table because it was warmer up off the floor.

She was allowed to listen because she was a princess and perhaps a future clan mother, and needed to know everything she could learn about the politics of the Six Nations Confederacy. And indeed the chief's gossip about the affairs taught her a great deal. But, as men will, they often fell to yarning. And then, oh, how she loved to hear the legends of the Indian past.

The Birth of Evil

This was how an old Oneida chief, himself nearly a hundred years old, said it had been in the beginning.

The Great Spirit created the world and all that lived in it, and they lived in peace and goodwill.

There came a time when the creatures who lived in the sea received a message. They were told that a beautiful maiden was about to be cast down into the waters among them, and that this maiden was about to become a mother.

The creatures of the seas did not know where they would put this young maiden because there was no land, they had a general discussion. The turtle who was kind and well-respected had a proposition, 'Let her land on my back, I am big and I am strong, she can

stay there forever.' The beautiful maiden did land on his back and her new home got larger and larger from the debris in the waters.

One day she heard voices and it was the voice of her unborn child. The next day she heard voices again and this time it was an argument: one voice said that he was restless, that he would force his birth and that his one and only purpose was to confuse the minds of people; the other voice said, let us be patient and obedient and fulfil our mission on earth. Right at that moment the restless one forced his way through the armpit of his mother – sin and evil was born and the mother died.

Dehganawihdeh

When Dehganawihdeh approached the village of the Mohawks, he sat beneath a tall tree gazing into the fire he had made. The chief warrior of the Mohawks came out to him to find out who he was and why he came to the Mohawk settlement. The stranger replied that the Great Creator, from whom all was created, had sent him to establish the Great Peace.

The chief warrior carried this message back to his people and everyone was summoned to a council. The Mohawks liked the idea of peace, and goodwill and an end to bloodshed, but they were wary of the stranger. They decided the man must give them a sign.

Let him climb to the top of that tall tree, to the highest branch, they said. We shall cut it down and let it fall over the cliff and into the falls. No one who has ever gone into the falls has survived. If the stranger lives to see sunrise we shall accept his message. And so it was.

Dehganawihdeh climbed to the highest branch and the Mohawks cut the tree. Dehganawihdeh fell over the cliff and into the falls. The Mohawks watched. He did not come up. The Mohawks waited. There was no sign of him, so they went back to the settlement.

Early the next morning the chief warrior went out of the settlement to the place of the tree, but no one was there. At a distance he saw smoke reaching to the skies. It was his duty to

investigate, for the chief warrior is charged with guarding the safety of his tribe and must be alert for anything unusual. So he went to see if the smoke was made by friend or foe.

The man sitting by the fire was the stranger who had gone over the falls. The chief warrior carried the news back to his tribe that the man was alive. The Mohawks brought in this man who was Dehganawihdeh to their settlement and gathered round him, and he talked to them of peace and power and goodwill, and as he talked the people of the Mohawk tribe accepted his divine message. Dehganawihdeh ordained and installed the lords of the confederacy. He said–'We have now completed arranging the system of our council, we shall hold our annual Confederate Council at the settlement of A-to-dal-ho, the capital or seat of the Government of the Five Nations'.

Then Dehganawihdeh said, 'Now I am you. Lords of the Confederate Nations shall plant a tree, Ska-renh-heh-se-go-wah (a tall and mighty tree), and we shall call it Jo-neh-rah-deh-sah-ko-wah (the tree of the great long leaves).

'This tree which we have planted shall shoot forth four great long white roots. These great long white roots shall shoot forth, one to the north, one to the south, one to the east and one to the west, and we shall place on the top of it O-donh-yoh (an eagle) which has great power of long vision and we shall transact all our business under the shade of this great tree. The meaning of this tree is Ka-yah-ne-renh-ko-wa (the Tree of Peace), and the nations of the earth shall see it and shall follow the root and arrive at this tree and the eagle on the top of the Great Tree is to watch the roots which extend to the north, to the south, to the east and to the west. The eagle will discover if any evil is approaching your confederacy and will scream and give alarm to all the Nations of the Confederacy.'

Dehganawihdeh then said: 'We shall now combine our power into one great power which is this confederacy. We shall now there-

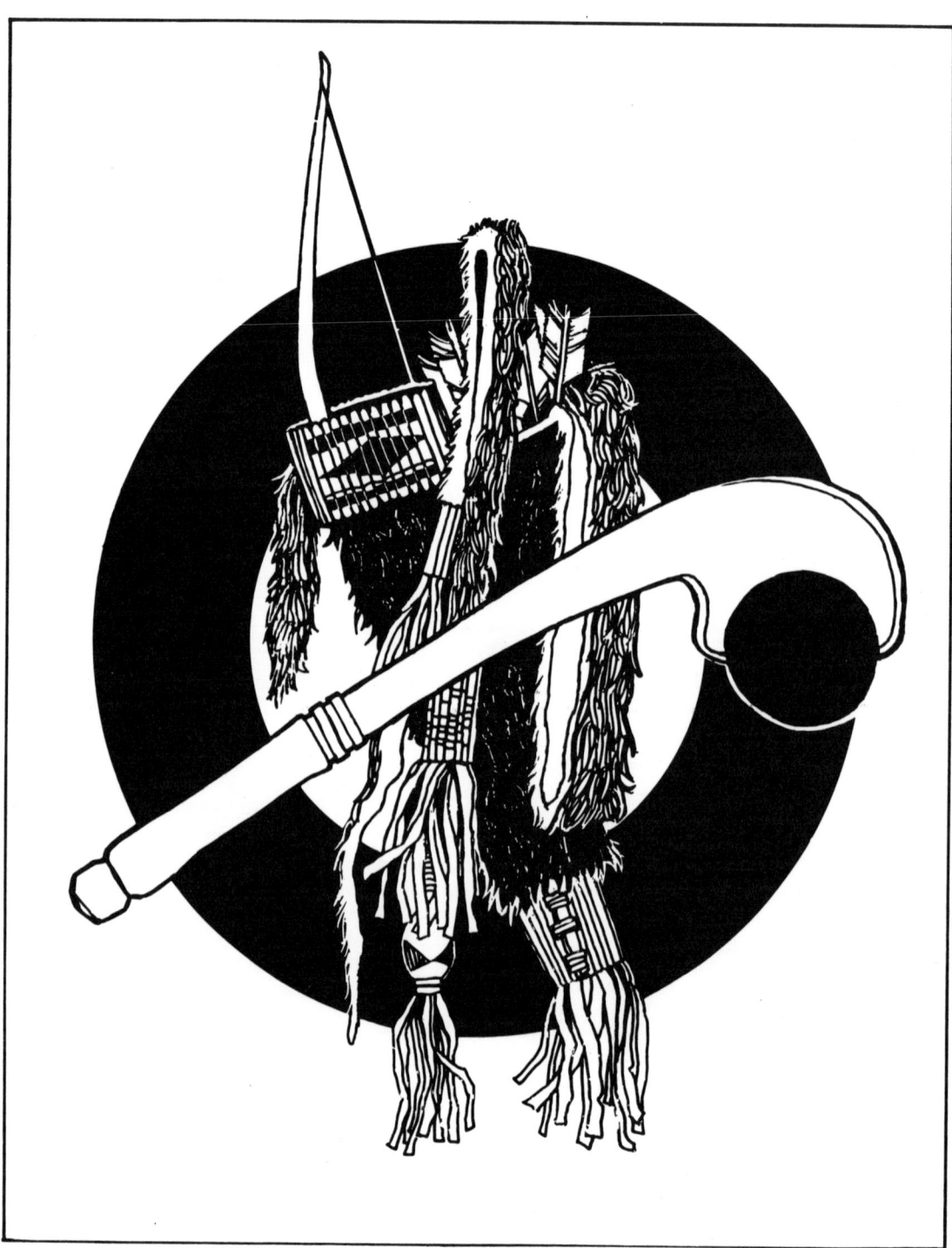

fore, symbolize the union of these powers by each nation contributing one arrow (each) which we shall tie up together in a bundle, so that when it is made completely and tied together, no one can bend or break it.' Dehganawihdeh said more–'We have now completed this union in securing one arrow from each nation. It is not good that one should be lacking or taken from the bundle, for it would weaken our power. It would be still worse if two arrows were taken and if three were taken, then anyone could break the remaining arrows in the bundle.

'We shall now therefore, tie this bundle of arrows together with deer's sinews which are strong, durable and lasting. This confederacy will be strong and unchangeable. This bundle of arrows signifies that all Lords of the Confederacy, Warriors, Women and Children have become united as one person. If any evil should befall us in the future, we shall stand or fall unitedly as one man. Your Lords shall be symbolized as Trees of the Five Confederate Nations. We therefore bind ourselves together by taking hold of each other's hands so firmly, forming a circle so strong by taking hold of each other's hands that if a tree should fall, it could not shake or break the circle–so that our people and grandchildren shall remain in the circle in security, peace and happiness. If any lord who is crowned with the emblem of deer's horns shall break through this circle of unity, his horns shall become fastened in the circle; and if he persists after warning from the Chief Matron, he shall go through the circle without his horns of authority, but shall remain in the circle after he has passed through. He shall no longer be a lord but shall be as an ordinary warrior, not qualified to fill any office.

'We have now completed everything in connection with the matter of peace and power. In reference to the disposal of all war weapons, we have decided to uproot the Great Tree, into which the weapons of war would be thrown and they would be swept away forever by the current so that the grandchildren would never see them and this they did.'

Dehganawihdeh then said: 'We have still

one matter left to be considered, that is with reference to the hunting grounds of our people from which they get their living. We shall only have one dish or bowl in which will be placed one beaver's tail. All shall have equal right, there shall be no knife to avoid the danger of bloodshed. This means that the hunting grounds shall have equal right to all people to hunt within its precincts.'

Dehganawihdeh continued: 'I shall now leave all matters in the hands of your lords. You are to work and carry out the principles of all I have laid before you for the welfare of your people. I now place the power in your hands to add to the rules and regulations whenever necessary. I now charge each of you lords never to disagree among yourselves. You are all of equal standing and of equal power. If you ever seriously disagree, you will disregard each other and while you are quarrelling, the White Lion (the fire dragon of discord) will come and take your rights and privileges away, then your grandchildren will suffer and be reduced to poverty and disgrace. If this should ever happen, then someone – who ever can – will climb the Great Tree and ascend to the top and look around over the landscape to see if there is any place or way to escape from the calamity of threatening poverty and disgrace. If he cannot see a way to escape, he will then look for a great swamp elm tree (A-ka-rah-ji-ko-wah) and there you will gather your heads together.

'If it should so occur that the heads of the confederacy should roll and wander away westward, other nations shall see your heads rolling and wandering away. They shall say, you belong to the confederacy, you were a proud and haughty people once. They shall kick the heads with scorn. They will go on their way and before they have gone far, they shall vomit blood which will be the penalty of other nations who will kick the heads of confederacy.

'There shall be another serious trouble. Whenever a person or persons of other nations shall cut any of the white roots of peace that grow from the Tree of Peace, a great trouble

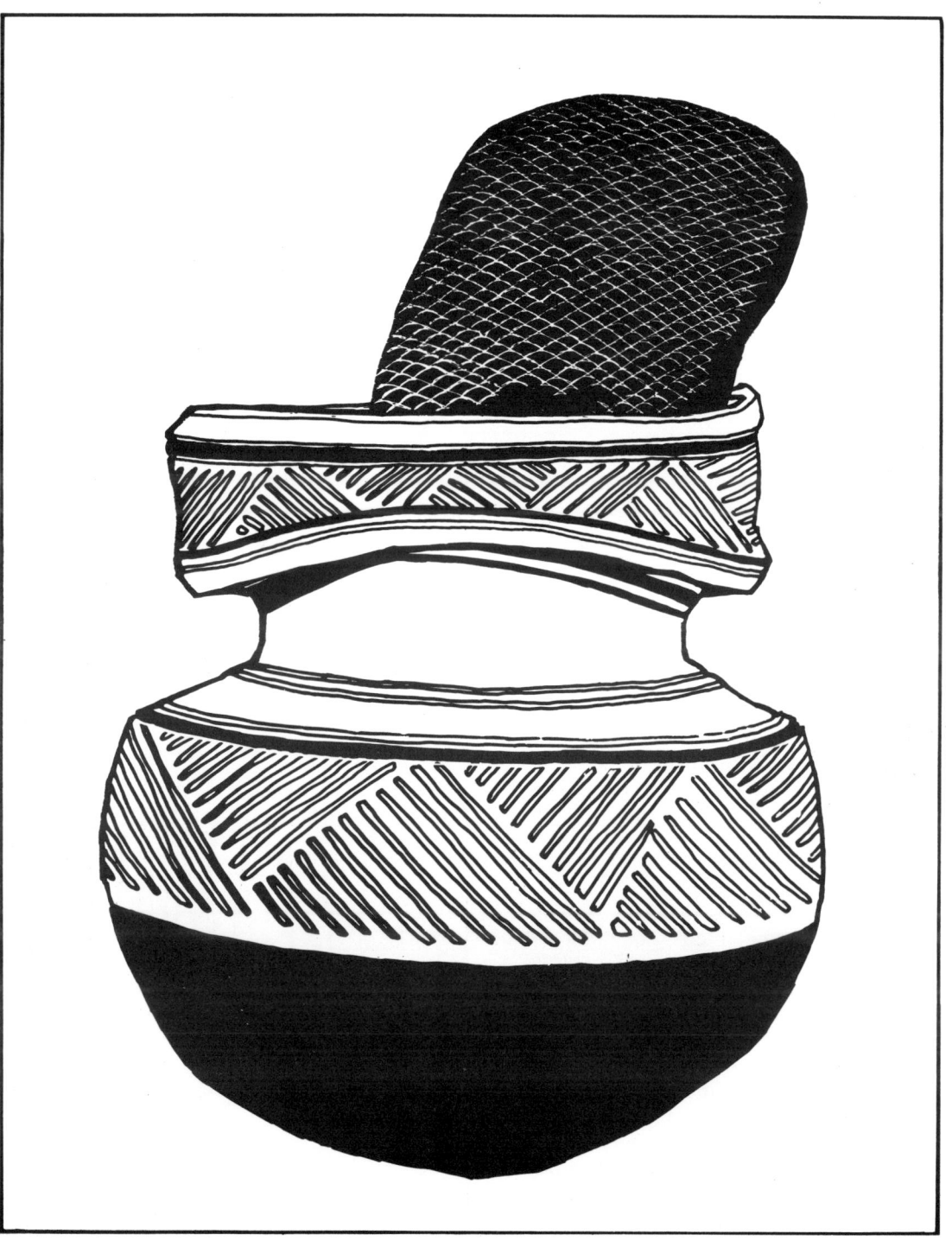

shall come into the seat of your Lords of Confederacy. I shall now charge each of the lords that your skin must be of the thickness of seven spreads of hands so that no matter how sharp a cutting instrument may be used, it will not penetrate through the thickness of your skin, signifying that the Lords of Confederacy must have patience and forbearance, goodwill in all their deliberations and never be disgraced by becoming angry.

'Lords of the different Nations of the Confederacy, I charge you to cultivate friendship, love and honour among your people. I have now fulfilled my duty and this confederacy shall last from generation unto generation, as long as the sun will continue to shine, the grass grows and waters run. There shall be no successor to my title and no man in the future shall be called by my name. If at any time through the negligence and carelessness of the lords, they fail to carry out the Constitution of the Confederacy and the people are reduced to great suffering, then I will return.'

And so the Five Nations Confederacy formed their council fire. The white wampum strings were the emblem of law when the Fire Keepers opened the council. The Onondaga lord held this string of wampum in his hand while he offered thanksgiving to the Great Spirit and while the council was in session, the strings of wampum were placed in their midst. When the council adjourned, the Fire Keeper picked up the wampum, held it in his hand and again offered thanksgiving and closed the council.

At every annual Confederate Council they smoke the Pipe of Peace. The Lords of the Confederacy define their obligations and position as follows:

If a lord is found guilty of willful murder, he will be deposed without warning by the Lords of the Confederacy and his horns, the emblem of power, will be handed back to the chief matron of his family and clan.

If a lord is guilty of rape, he will be deposed without warning by the Lords of the Confederacy and his horns, the emblem of power, will be handed back to the chief matron of his family and clan.

If a lord is guilty of theft, he will be deposed.

If a lord is guilty of unjustly opposing the object of decisions and showing disrespect for his brother lords, he will be approached by the chief matron of his family and urged to desist from such evil practices. If the lord still refuses to listen and obey, a warrior of his clan will approach him to desist from his evil ways. If the lord again refuses to obey, the Chief Warrior shall take the deer's horn from his head – his emblem of power – and give it back to the chief matron. Then the matron will select and appoint another warrior of her family and crown him. A new lord is created in the place of the one deposed.

The lords of each of the Confederate Nations shall have one Chief Warrior. His duty shall be to carry messages through the dense forests between the settlements, and in the absence of the lord through illness he shall act in his place of council.

The Chief Warriors of the Five Nations Confederacy are as follows: Mohawks, Senecas, Onondagas, Oneidas and Cayugas.

When a lord is deposed and the emblem of power is taken from him, he shall not be allowed to sit in council or hold an office again. If a lord is deceased, the Chief Matron and the warriors of the family clan shall nominate another warrior of the same clan to succeed the deceased. If the family and clan in which a lordship is vested shall become extinct, the Confederate Council will consider the matter, nominate and appoint a successor from any family of the brother lords of the deceased. If a lord becomes ill, the Lords of the Confederacy shall visit the dying lord and take his deer's horns off his head and place them beside the wall so that if by the will of the Great Spirit he recovers from his illness, he will again take up his crown of deer's horns and resume the duties of a lord. During his illness, a string of black wampum is hung at the head of his bed, and if he dies, anyone belonging to his clan will take this string of black wampum and announce his death to the whole circle of the confederacy. In case of the death of a lord, his colleagues, the chiefs, will remove his crown of deer's horns.

Thus were the Mohawks the elders of the confederacy, first in intelligence and at the council fire. They were called the 'fountain of good works', and were the sponsors of crucial matters in the council.

After this Dehganawihdeh left to carry his message to the other Indian tribes.

Hiawatha

Dehganawihdeh went to the home of Hiawatha, who ate humans for his meals. He climbed to the top of Hiawatha's house and sat beside the smoke hole and waited for him to come home. Deganawihdeh saw him coming at a distance. He was carrying a human body.

Hiawatha entered the house and put the body into the black iron pot that hung over the fire. As Hiawatha looked into the pot, Dehganawihdeh peered down through the smoke hole. Hiawatha saw the reflection in the water and thought it was his own. He had seen his reflection in the water many times, but this time it was different—there in the water was the face of a noble, kind and honest man. Hiawatha went outside to ponder about the face. How wise and kind it looked. It wasn't the face of one who ate humans. Yet he was alone, so it must be his own reflection. Somehow he felt different. He wanted to be kind and wise like the face. So he went in and took the black pot and emptied it outside. At once he felt good, so good that he felt like laughing out loud. He wondered what it would sound like if he laughed out loud.

Just then Dehganawihdeh climbed down from the roof, and Hiawatha told him what happened. Dehganawihdeh said, 'Now you have repented of your evil. I will name you Hiawatha which means He-who-combs, for you shall be the one to comb the snakes out of the wizard's hair.' He placed upon Hiawatha's head the antlers of the deer, which signify the power of authority.

Dehganawihdeh said, 'When I have completed my mission on earth, I shall place the antlers of authority upon the heads of the men I shall ordain, and it shall be an emblem to all nations that this is the new order of peace,

power and goodwill that I was sent to accomplish on earth.'

When Hiawatha first visited the wizard A-to-tar-ho, he could not persuade him to take hold of the message of peace, even though A-to-tar-ho's tribe, the Onondagas had already accepted it. Hiawatha tried three times to approach him, and three times he failed, for A-to-tar-ho had power over the lake that must be crossed to reach his home. Even some of his own Onondaga tribesmen had been drowned trying to reach A-to-tar-ho's shore by canoe.

Hiawatha withdrew in sorrow. One day while meditating in the deep forest he heard the voice of A-to-tar-ho in the air all about him. It was a voice like thunder, and it called again and again, 'Hiawatha, Hiawatha'. The air was filled with the sound. Hiawatha knew something had happened to his family.

Soon after he returned to his house, his three daughters sickened and died. Hiawatha's head was bowed with grief and he could not be comforted. His people went to him and tried to rouse him from his grief, but they failed. So they made up a game. They made a ball and gathered sticks, put crooks in the sticks and netted them with vines. They chose two teams of men, each one having a goal to guard. They began to play. So was lacrosse invented, to console Hiawatha in his great grief. The Indians called their game the Cross Sticks.

While the Indians were playing the Cross Sticks, a great bird dropped from the skies and the players stopped their game to pursue it. In the excitement Hiawatha's wife was trampled to death. This, too, was the work of A-to-tar-ho, the wizard.

Hiawatha left his home and the graves of his family. He came to a lake and the lake was full of geese. When he approached, the geese lifted the water in their bills and Hiawatha walked over the dry lake bed.

As he walked, he found on the lake bottom shells, which he picked up and threaded on three strings to mark his grief. He held the

strings in his hand and thought that if anyone were burdened with a grief like his, the strings would console him. He repeated this over and over, and the shells on the wampum became words of truth and comfort to wash away tears and sorrow.

So began the condolence ceremony with the wampum strings that even today is used by the chiefs of the confederacy when a chief dies. It is performed on the tenth day after death, for the time of mourning is ten days.

A-to-tar-ho, the wizard

A-to-tar-ho, who was a very powerful wizard, lived on the edge of a lake. His evil powers gave him full command of the lake, and no bird or beast or human dared approach him. When they tried, A-to-tar-ho caused the waves of the lake to dash them to death against the rocks.

When birds flew over his domain he caused them to fall dead at his feet. A-to-tar-ho loved disorder and hated peace. He had a twisted body, and his head was covered over with snakes.

Dehganawihdeh, with his own supernatural powers, was able to cross the lake to A-to-tar-ho and he found the wizard sitting on a rock by the water. When Dehganawihdeh spoke of peace and goodwill, the words fell on deaf ears and a dark mind. A-to-tar-ho's only reply was a bloodthirsty cry that echoed far into the settlements of the other tribes, bringing terror to all who heard him. Dehganawihdeh said, 'I shall come again and I shall bring someone who will comb the snakes out of your hair.'

One day Dehganawihdeh took Hiawatha to see A-to-tar-ho. They approached the wizard slowly, chanting the peace chant as they came, and A-to-tar-ho fell under its spell. Now he could hear with a clear mind.

Hiawatha held the wampum in his hand, and explained to A-to-tar-ho the words of the law that it represented. As he listened, A-to-tar-ho remembered the people he had killed and the ones he had enjoyed tormenting, and

he heard their cries. His past life was like an open book in his hand. Page after page was filled with his cruelty. When he had seen enough, when he could stand the cries of the tormented no longer, he begged for peace and mercy. Hiawatha had combed the snakes of evil out of his hair.

Dehganawihdeh saw true repentance. He called A-to-tar-ho and placed on his head the horns of the deer and ordained him the hereditary chief of the Onondagas and the one to cast the deciding vote in any dispute in the council of the Six Nations Confederacy.

The Tree of Peace
The message of peace, power and goodwill was accepted by the Mohawks, the Oneidas, and Onondagas, the Cayugas and the Senecas.

After Dehganawihdeh had ordained and installed the Lords of the Confederacy, he said: 'We have now arranged the system of our council. We shall hold our annual council at the settlement of A-to-tar-ho, which will be the seat of government of the Five Nations.'

Then Dehganawihdeh said, 'Now, Lords of the Confederate Nations, I and you shall plant a tree, Ska-renh-heh-se-go-wah (a tall and mighty tree), and we shall call it Jo-ne-rah-deh-sah-ko-wah (the tree of the great long leaves). This tree which we have planted shall put forth four great white roots, one to the north, one to the south, one to the east and one to the west. And we shall place on top of it Oh-don-yonh (the eagle), who has the power of long vision, and we shall transact all our business under the shade of this great tree.

'This tree is Ka-yah-ne-renh-ko-wa, the Tree of Peace and its meaning is that the nations of the earth may see it and follow the roots and arrive at this place. You will receive them and seat them in the midst of your confederacy.' And so it happened, for the Tuscarora followed the roots to the Tree of Peace in the eighteenth century. Thus the Five Nations became Six Nations, though the Tuscaroras have no vote.

Dehganawihdeh further said: 'The meaning of the eagle at the top of the great tree is to discover any evil that might threaten the confederacy. The eagle will watch the roots that stretch to the north and the south and the east and the west and will scream and give alarm if evil approaches. We shall now combine our power into one great power which is this confederacy. We shall now therefore symbolize the union of these powers. Each nation shall contribute one arrow, and we shall bind the arrows together in a bundle, and when the bundle is made, no one can bend or break it. It is not good that even one arrow should be lacking or taken from the bundle, for that would weaken our power. Still worse would be the taking of two arrows, and if three were taken then anyone could break what was left of the bundle.

'We shall now therefore bind this bundle with deer's sinew's which are strong and lasting, and the confederacy shall endure. Now the lords of confederacy and the warriors and the women and the children are united as one person. If any evil should befall, we shall stand as one man. You lords shall be the trees of the five confederate nations and we shall therefore bind ourselves together in a circle by joining hands so firmly that if a tree should fall upon it the circle could not shake or break.

'If any lord who is crowned with the deer's horns should break through this circle of unity, his horns shall fasten themselves in the circle, to prevent him. If, even after the warning of the Chief Matron, he should persist, he shall go through the circle without his horns of authority. But he will remain in the circle even after he has passed through, though he will remain as an ordinary warrior and not as a lord, and will not qualify again to fill any office. We have now completed everything in connection with the matter of peace and power.'

Saying that, Dehganawihdeh uprooted the Tree of Peace. Beneath it was a great current of water flowing away to unknown regions. Into this cavern he threw the hatchets and war clubs and all the weapons of war so that the children and grandchildren should never see them. Then he replaced the tree and the Great Peace was established.

Then Dehganawihdeh said: 'We have one matter left to be considered and that concerns the hunting grounds by which we live. We shall only have one dish and in it will be one beaver's tail. All shall have equal right. Lest there be bloodshed, there shall be no knife. This signifies that all our people shall have equal right to hunt in the hunting grounds.

'I now leave all matters in the hands of your lords. I now place the power in your hands to add rules to this code when they are necessary. I now charge you lords never to disagree among yourselves. If you quarrel, the fire-dragon of discord will come and take away your rights and privileges, and your grand-children will suffer, and know poverty and disgrace. If this should happen then someone, whoever can, will climb the great tree and look over the landscape to see if there is any place or way to escape from the threatening calamity. If there is no way, he must then look for a great swamp elm tree, A-ka-rah-ji-ko-wah, and there you will gather your heads together.

'If the heads of the confederacy should ever roll and wander away westward, other nations will see it and will say "you were a proud and haughty people once," and they will kick the heads with acorns. And they will go on their way. But before they have gone far they will vomit blood; for that is the penalty for other nations that kick the heads of the confederacy.

'If anyone should cut any of the white roots of peace that grow from the Tree of Peace, a great trouble will come. I therefore charge you lords, your skin must be the thickness of seven spreads of hands. Thus, no matter how sharp a cutting instrument be used, it will not pene-trate the thickness of your skins. The lords of the confederacy must have patience and forbearance, and goodwill in all their deliberations. They must never be disgraced by growing angry.

'Lords of the nations of the confederacy, I charge you to cultivate friendship, love and honor among your people. This confederacy shall last from generation unto generation, as long as the sun shines, the grass grows and the waters run. I have now fulfilled my duty. There

shall be no successor to my title, and no man shall be called by my name. But if at any time the lords, through neglect or carelessness, fail to carry out the constitution of the confederacy, then will I return.'

The Six Nations Indians put the founding date of the confederacy at 1390. From it came the inspiration for the American colonies to unite by example, and the constitution of the United States is based on its unwritten code. The confederacy has often been described as the first working United Nations.

Status

The children of the Six Nations were not at any time ignorant of their status. Our fathers have taught us that the constitution of the Five Nations was the Tree of Peace, Power and Goodwill, brought to us by the Supreme Being, Dehganawihdeh.

He wrote this sacred message upon the hearts and minds of each individual Onhgivehonweh (Indian). A child who is an heiress to the divine mission of chieftainship must live under the golden rule of the Great Tree of Peace under which the lords of our confederacy was ordained.

When a male child is heir to the chieftainship, he is well prepared and capable to take his place as a lord of the confederacy. He must have faith in the Creator, be true and honest to his people, and forever faithful to the government of his nation. The Great Tree of Peace shall exist until he, Dehganawihdeh, shall come again.

Principal Chiefs of the Mohawk Tribe

Bear Clan
Dehennakarine
Aghstawenserontha
Shosgoharowane

Turtle Clan
Dekarihaokenh
Ayonkwatha
Sadehgarihwadeh

Wolf Clan
Sharinhowane
Devonnhehgonh
Ohrenregowah

INDIAN STORIES

Forbidden Voice had never heard about Santa Claus until one day her parents had taken her to town for a pair of new shoes. There she became friends with two white girls her own age. They told her it was Christmas Eve, the night before Christmas, it was the night when they hung their stockings up and Santa Claus came during the night and filled them with beautiful presents. He came in his magic sled drawn by his magic reindeer, high up in the clouds and with his pack of toys came down through the chimney and visited all little boys and girls who hung their stockings up beside the chimney fire. Forbidden Voice could not understand how this could happen, for in her own life there was much magic but never one like Santa Claus and his magic reindeer. She became very happy as she listened to her two new friends.

One of them said she was going to get a new doll for Christmas, and pointed out the one she wanted in the shop window. It was beautiful. It had shining yellow hair and blue eyes and pretty lace clothes and it was bigger than any doll Forbidden Voice had ever seen – the size of a real baby.

That night when Forbidden Voice came home she was feverish with excitement. Was Santa Claus going to bring her a lot of brand-new toys, too? she asked. Her mother explained gently that Santa Claus was the white man's way of making children happy. 'But', she said, 'we real people, we Indians, are happy because we have a Creator who created all things to make us so. He dwells in the sun, moon and stars, and in the sunshine and rain that makes things grow. That is more than enough, and so we have been told by our ancient forefathers always to be happy and thankful.'

The little girl picked up her two old corn-husk dolls thoughtfully and carried them to bed, where she was soon fast asleep. That night she had a dream.

She dreamed she saw Santa Claus with a huge pack of toys standing beside the stocking she had hung up. Not wanting to disturb him, she closed her eyes, but when she opened them again he was gone and in her stocking was the

doll from the store window, except that its face was like the face of one of the little white girls she had talked to in town. Beside the stocking was a doll carriage and also a toy dog. She took the doll and hugged it tightly in her arms. She picked up the toy dog and hugged it too.

Suddenly she heard loud sobs. It was her own dog, Tori, howling pitifully just under her window. Then there was sobbing all around, and when she turned she saw her two cornhusk dolls crying as if their hearts would break.

Then, as she watched, the cornhusk dolls began to move. They jumped to the floor and, with a war cry, began a ceremonial dance. At the same instant, other cornhusk dolls came in swarms like bees, through the cracks of the walls and ceiling and floors, until the room was filled. As they danced to the tom-tom, they trampled the doll carriage to bits. The toy dog dropped from her arms. The beautiful doll with its real-life face began to shrivel. Then, one by one, the cornhusk dolls returned through the cracks they had come in by and the room was empty, except for the whimpering of Tori under her window.

When the little girl woke the next morning her two cornhusk dolls were safe beside her on the bed and as she hugged them she vowed that no white man's toy would ever take their place.

Forbidden Voice hadn't met many white people, mind you, and when she thought of them she thought of them as something to be feared. They were all mixed up in her mind with the punishing angels the white minister talked about in church.

Later, when she knew more of them, she saw that she had as many bones as any white person, and a body to do her bidding and a mind to think with. What she thought, then, was that Santa Claus was just a white man's superstition. But her people had their own myths and superstitions and these suited Forbidden Voice better.

Because of her dream she particularly treasured the Legend of the Corn. But indeed she treasured them all.

The legend of the corn

Her mother told her this, after Forbidden Voice had her dream of the cornhusk dolls.

Man-beings were not created to kill, but to do the will of the Creator, for all things on earth were created for a divine purpose.

The corn that grew tall and stately had many missions. The kernel was for food. The dry meal gave sustenance to the hunters who travelled many miles in search of game. The flour, made by pounding, was molded into round cakes and put into boiling water and used for bread. The husks were used to stuff mattresses, or, braided and sewn together, made into scatter mats. The husks were also used to make cornhusk dolls. The stalks of the corn were carried to the woods to feed the wild animals, who are the brothers of the Indian.

For each and every different use the Indian burned the sacred tobacco, sending his thanks to the Creator. In return it was given to the Indian to understand the voice of the corn, when it warned him of approaching danger. When the corn crossed its stocks like sword-blades and bowed its head to the earth, the Indians knew that trouble threatened.

Thus it was that one day an Indian runner passed a field of corn. The day was cloudless and the sky was blue. But as he passed, the cornstalks waved their blades like long arms beckoning him, and the runner understood their message. He ran to his tribe and told them to come, and when they followed him to the cornfield and were gathered round him, suddenly all became still. In the silence came a voice and this is what the voice said: 'When the end is near, I will grow no taller than two feet. My cobs will be dwarfs, a third of their usual size. Then is the time to store away all the food I yield. It will be enough for all who have not broken faith with us, who are created by the Creator. The end will be near but no harm will befall you.'

The Indians believe this.

Man, the dog's master

Before death came among the people, the dog lived like a human being, and had a voice like a

human's. His first duty was to warn his master at the approach of danger. The people had three dogs in their camp. Each day the dogs went into the woods in search of game. When they had found it they returned to tell the men where to hunt.

One day in the woods the three dogs were approached by the enemy. The enemy tempted them with food and false promises, and the dogs forgot their duty and for the sake of greed answered whatever the enemy wanted to know. They told the secret entrance to the camp.

Late that night the camp was attacked by way of the secret entrance. Many people were killed. The bodies of women and children and old men were scattered everywhere. The ones who lived could not understand why the rest lay so cold and still. Death was still a mystery.

For three days and nights they watched, waiting for their loved ones to rise from their slumber. On the fourth day the head men of the tribes held a council. The attack had come from the secret entrance. But the secret entrance was supposed to be well guarded by the three dogs. The dogs were called to be questioned.

Finally one of the dogs admitted that all three had been tricked by fine food and excellent promises. The three dogs rolled on the ground and begged for mercy.

The medicine man who was the people's leader rose to his feet slowly. He pointed to the dead and speaking solemnly he said to the dogs: 'From this time you shall never talk again, though you can hear and understand. When you want to be heard, you will bark, and you will bark for your food. This is your punishment for the wrong you have done'.

The dogs' punishment was fulfilled, but in spite of it he is still the guardian and friend of his master.

The six sons

This is a story handed down for centuries among the Six Nations Indians.

A man had six sons. When they were young, they grew restless and wanted to go out into

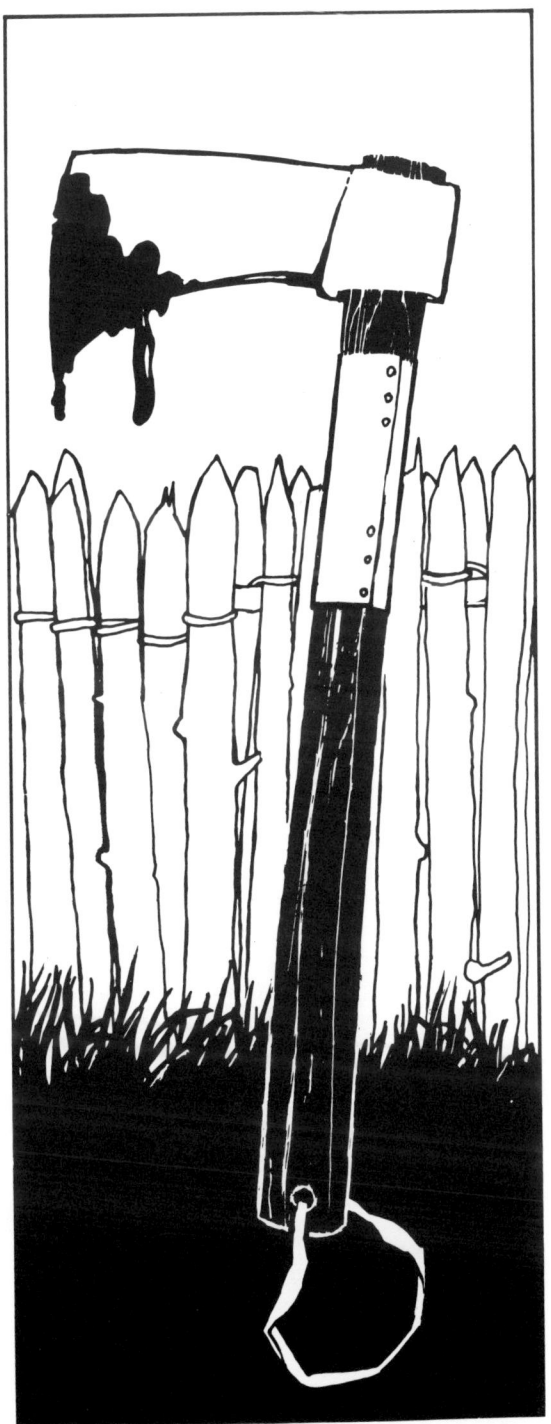

the world. Their father pleaded with them at least to go one at a time, so the eldest left home first.

As he said farewell to his father and brothers, he told them that if he did not return in a month they would know that he could not come. A month passed and he did not come. They waited three days, and then the second son said he was going to look for his brother. If he did not return in a month they would know that he, too, could not come. He did not return. The third and fourth and fifth sons went likewise and now only the sixth and youngest was left at home.

One night he had a dream and the following day he told his father that he was going in search of his brothers and that he had seen in his dream what he must take with him. The old man asked him what that might be and the boy replied: 'A small bag of flour made from scorched corn pounded fine; a brew made from live-forever roots and the whips of the twisted tree, a small jar of live firebugs, and a bow and

arrow dipped in graveyard dirt.'

After everything was gathered and prepared he said good-bye to his father and left. He found the trail his five brothers had left, for they had marked it well. It went deep into the forest, and as he walked along it suddenly he heard the deep roar of a lion. He took out the brew made from live-forever roots and the whips of the twisted tree and drank some of it. It made him as strong as ten men and when the lion bounded out at him he took its jaws and tore them apart and the lion fell dead at his feet. As he looked down at it he saw beside the path the bones of his eldest brother.

So he went on. When he got hungry, he took out his bag of scorched meal and put one morsel in his mouth. It was enough to give him strength for a whole day and night.

The trail led deeper and deeper into the woods, and all of a sudden he found himself caged in a spider web as thick as a tangle of ropes. As he struggled he saw the bodies of his other four brothers.

But the youngest was strong with the strength of the scorched meal, so he burst his way out of the bonds and went on cautiously down the trail. Soon he heard laughter like the roar of the thunder. Coming towards him on the trail was a giant with his head thrown back in mirth. The giant said, 'I am glad you got this far. I have not had fresh meat for a long time. I shall eat you first, and then your brothers who are safe in my keeping.'

The young man got his jar of firebugs and opened it. The firebugs flew everywhere, confusing the giant with their winking lights. Then the young man took a pinch of graveyard dust and threw it in the giant's eyes, to blind him. Then the young man seized his bow and poisoned arrow and shot the giant through the heart. The giant fell to the ground and spiders came from everywhere to feast on him.

The young man turned back and found his four brothers entangled in the cobwebs, and released them, and laid their bodies in a row on the ground.

Then he fetched the bones of his eldest brother and laid them beside the others. He took the brew made of live-forever roots and the whips of the twisted tree and rubbed his brothers, covering every part of their bodies. When he detected signs of life he quickly put into their mouths a portion of the scorched corn meal. In a few moments they had revived completely. After they had sung the ancient restoration chant they all returned to their father.

There was great rejoicing.

Bear Day

Fifty groundhogs invited fifty bears to help plan a party. When the bears got there they discovered that the groundhogs were holding the party to celebrate Groundhog Day. The bears were very angry and said the day was really supposed to be Bear Day. They said that in the beginning the people had made a bargain with the bears. The bears understood the seasons, and they knew the time at the end of the winter when their honey supplies were running low. If the bears would agree to tell the people when winter was almost over, so they could tap the maple trees for syrup (a substitute for honey), then the day would be named in their honor.

The groundhogs argued that everyone had forgotten about the promise, if it ever had existed, and the day had been called Ground-hog Day for so long it would be foolish to change. The bears argued back that the groundhogs didn't like honey and wouldn't know what the right day was, because they weren't as sophisticated as the bears.

The meeting was getting out of hand, so a wise old bear suggested they have the party first and settle the dispute later. This is what they did, and so the question of whose day it was was never settled.

But the squirrel, who was not even invited to the party, gave it as his opinion that both sides were silly anyway. Neither was as important as he. While the groundhog and the bear slept the time away, didn't he, the squirrel, warn the earth people what kind of winter to prepare for?

The chickens talked
Granny was an old lady who had once had nine daughters. One by one the daughters had died, and now she had only her husband left. She was very lonely, so one day her husband bought her three chickens at an auction sale to keep her company. She put them in a box and talked to them all day.

One day the hunters brought her husband home from the woods, ill and unconscious, and in spite of everything she did for him, he died the next day. Now she was all alone and that night, after the funeral, she sat by the fire and wept, remembering how once her home had been filled with life and laughter.

She cried harder and harder until suddenly she heard a voice saying, 'Don't cry. You are not alone.' But there was nothing there but the chickens who by now had grown into hens. Granny went to bed and all night long she dreamed of the way it used to be when her

family was alive and all together.

When she got up the next morning, she found, to her surprise, that someone had cleaned and tidied the house the way her daughters used to do, and every morning after that she awoke to a clean house. Sometimes in the night she thought she could hear voices but she paid no attention and she never thought of the hens.

One day when Granny was feeding them, the hens jostled the bowl out of her hands by accident and it smashed on the floor. It was a bowl her husband had given her and she was very angry and chased them out to the barn with her broom.

She left them there for three days without food and water and by the end of that time the hens decided she did not deserve their help any more. They would clean no houses and give no eggs and would sit on their nests without making a sound and never get in her way again.

One night the hens heard a great crash in the house. But true to their decision they did not go to look. All the next day there was silence from the house, but the following night they heard a noise like a groan. With that they flew to the window to look. There was their mis-tress under the corner of a heavy cupboard that had fallen. They forgot their hurt and anger.

They flew into the house and tugged at the cupboard till it moved. They helped Granny to get up, stoked the fire in the stove to warm the house, and made hot soup for the old woman to eat.

Then she knew who had cleaned the house. And she knew she had company in her loneli-ness. And she never chased the hens out to the barn again.

Laughing Water
Forbidden Voice loved to hear the legends of long ago, especially about the Maid of the Laughing Water. A young Indian brave took his beautiful young bride for a ride in his canoe, he loved to sing the native songs of his ancestors, the peace chant which Hiawatha

sang for the great Onondaga chief (A-to-tar-ho) as he combed all the snakes out of his hair. He also taught his wife to sing the lullaby his own mother sang for him when he was little. Soon his wife would sing the same lullaby to put her own baby to sleep.

The native chants fascinated her, the songs seemed to rise from the earth lingering for a moment in the skyworld and then upward to the mansions above where the Creator abides.

The earth chant carried peace to the human heart, consolation to the tired hunter, wise counsel to the rulers of the man-beings and a heavenly melody for the children, as the pathway to the heaven world is full of the prints of little feet.

The chant of the skyworld is of thanksgiving for the sun, the moon and the stars who give protection, guidance and sustenance to all man-beings.

The chant to the mansions above wherein the Creator abides is a full and deep submission of a contrite heart, and the Great Spirit is the king above all kings.

There is also a chant for the beautiful birds that sing heavenly messages to the fairies who dance and give thanks before the break of day.

One evening the young wife became very restless, the time was close at hand to give birth to her baby, and she pleaded with her young Indian brave to take her out in the canoe. She wanted to hear once more the chants of their ancestors, they gave her great peace.

Hand in hand they went down to the water's edge where the canoe was, the water was still and calm as they climbed into the canoe. They glided along as he softly sang the native chants of their ancestors, unconscious of time and place. A wind had come up and carried them to the rapids, and the Indian knew only too well that soon they would be caught and dashed over the falls to the rocks below. In spite of his desperate efforts to turn back he knew he could not make it. He glanced at his young wife, she smiled and he knew that she

was at the point of giving birth to their child. He grabbed her and held her tight as they were swept over the falls, but just then a strange thing happened – a kind fairy whose home was in a crevice of the rocks darted out and saved the baby which happened to be a beautiful girl.

She took the baby girl to her home in the crevice of the rocks, she loved her and taught her the mysteries of the great waterfalls of the world – it was the little girl's playground and the resting place of her beautiful young parents. When the moon is full and bright, voices can be heard above the roar of the waterfall and the songs of the peace chants of long ago sound loud and clear. The condolence chant of Hiawatha shall quiet forever the sorrows of mankind.

The kind fairy would smile for she knew that Laughing Water was with her parents. In ancient times people have seen her with her long black locks and silvery gown, standing erect in her canoe, with her paddle hoisted high above her head and her laughter louder than the roar of the water as she gracefully glides over the falls. People have said that Laughing Water still lives with the kind fairy in the crevice of the rocks.

The legend of the tree toad

The legend of the tree toad is about an Indian girl who never did anything she was told to do. Her mother was very sad, because this was the only child she had and she loved her very much. At times the little girl wished she could be a nice girl and almost tried to be, but it was impossible.

One night she put on her best dress and shoes. Quite contrary to her mother's protests, she went outside and made mud pies. It was right after a rain storm, and the little girl walked in and out of the house, and tracked up her mother's clean floor. Her mother began to cry, while the little girl with a grin on her face walked into the next room. She heard a tapping noise at the window, and there sat a cute little toad nodding his head and saying 'Let me in,

you bad girl, I want to talk to you.' The little girl went to the door, opened it, and he hopped in. 'Who are you?' she asked. 'I am a tree toad and I can change my colour to suit myself', he said and jumped on the white window whereupon he became white, then he jumped on the green chair and became green. The little girl clapped her hands saying, 'I want to be like you' over and over again. The tree toad replied, 'Your wish is granted, but don't cry to me afterwards. You always have your way so enjoy yourself.'

The little girl made a curtsy to him with an ugly sneer on her face, and she remained that way. Then the tree toad gave her a mirror for keeps so she could see what she looked like, and she looked at herself and saw the ugly sneer on her face. She tried to smile but there were ugly fangs protruding from her mouth, she tried to think of nice things but she had been bad for so long that she could not think of anything nice. Just then her mother called her to come for lunch. She obeyed immediately –which was unusual–and her fangs disappeared.

After lunch her mother asked her to wash the dishes, and the little girl went into a tantrum. She remembered the mirror, looked at herself and saw that there were snakes crawling in and out of her hair. She became frantic and ran into the kitchen and started washing the dishes. The little girl began to feel good, she looked into the mirror, she was beautiful, she danced for joy. But it was hard to break the habit of being disobedient, and when her mother called her to change her dress, the girl became so angry she splashed muddy water over her dress and tore the sleeve right off. Her mother began to cry again–big drops of tears fell to the floor. The little Indian girl looked defiantly at her mother, as she saw the drops of tears getting bigger and bigger until they made a puddle which reached the top of her shoes. Up to her knees, higher and higher it came, and then there was water up to her chin. She knew that she would be drowned in her mother's tears, and she ran to her mother gasping for breath and screaming, 'Forgive me mother I shall never be disobedient again.' The mother forgave her daughter.

GHOSTS

An encounter with the Hand
Apparitions foretell the future
Good and evil spirits

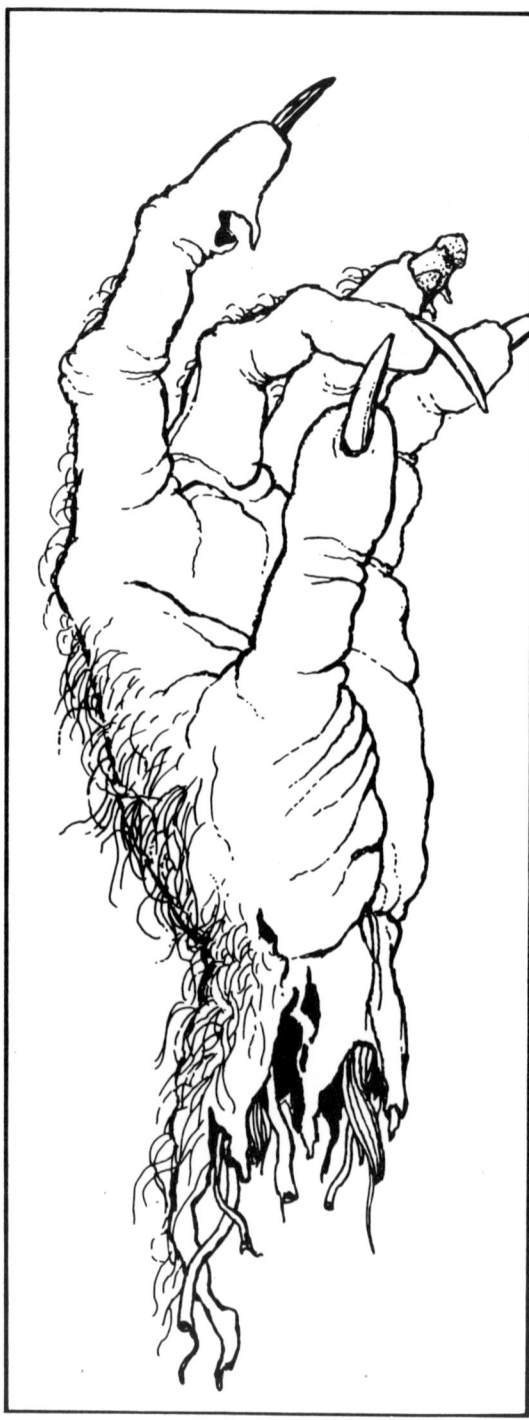

When Forbidden Voice was six, her teen-age brother disappeared during the night. He came back the next day but he was very quiet, and he had a black eye. Forbidden Voice pestered him to say where he had gone and what had happened, and this is what he told her.

He and another boy had decided they hated the long hours of work they had to put in working on a farm–they wanted to have fun like the boys who had money in their pockets and sneaked into the nearby taverns on week-ends. One of these cutups was now in jail, but the boys had decided that even jail was more exciting than their own hard life. So they saved up their pennies and planned to run away.

On the night they chose, they sneaked out of their homes late at night and began walking. They walked for miles and miles, and after a while a storm blew up. They were still in familiar territory and they knew there was a barn nearby, so they decided to shelter there for the rest of the night. At daylight they would be on their way again, for they had made up their minds to go to some far-away place where there would be no cows to milk or pigs to feed.

They knew people would be out looking for them, so when they got inside the barn they climbed up to the hayloft, took off their shoes, and settled down. Still whispering so they wouldn't be heard and wondering who would be the first to notice their absence, they drifted off to sleep.

Suddenly the other boy jumped up screaming 'Help me!' He seemed to be struggling with something on his face. Just as the little girl's brother got to him, the boy jerked the something away and threw it as hard as he could. It flew right back as if it were alive, slapped the brother's face and clung to his cheek. It was an unattached hand. The brother tried to fight it off but it had powerful fingers and it kept hitting his head and face. When he beat it off for a moment it flew to the other boy, and it kept flying from one face to the other till the boys tumbled down from the loft and ran out of the barn. They ran all the way home with the hand slapping at them, and it was

broad daylight before they noticed they had left their shoes back at the barn.

Forbidden Voice had already heard about the Hand. All the Indian children had, though they were too afraid of it to talk about it much. It went after naughty children and unruly teen-agers. Later, when she was older, Forbidden Voice heard hundreds of tales about the Hand and everyone spoke of it with a shiver. Old men could still remember its touch, for it was ice cold.

So Indian children never went out after dark. If they had a chance to visit playmates in the evenings, their mothers went with them. No one wanted the Hand to come after him.

There was something even more terrible and frightening called the Naked Leg. It was a long time before Forbidden Voice understood that the Naked Leg was for grownups who sinned against the stern morality of the confederacy, and for prostitutes. She had heard an old man tell about it one time, and he had said it would haunt and even kill a person. He said it made

the decisions for people at crossroads, and he said it was a crotch with two legs that were alive.

Her brother's story about the Hand was the first ghost story that Forbidden Voice had heard that had happened to someone she really knew. But afterwards there were to be many. A neighbor would come running in the middle of the night, terrified because there had been knocking at the door and when she had opened it no one was there; or there would be sounds every night from an empty room; or the door of a sick room would keep swinging silently open when no one had gone near it. Once, when someone in the family was ill, a plate she was carrying to him shattered in Forbidden Voice's hand. The man died soon after. Because such things happened so often all around her, and to so many of the other Indians, Forbidden Voice believed they had meaning. She believed that no matter how dark and terrible they were, they had a mean-ing and she believed that sooner or later you

learned what the meaning was. Though the ghost stories often frightened Forbidden Voice she couldn't help listening to them.

Apparition
This happened to an Indian schoolteacher on the reserve, who was returning to her boarding house in a horse and buggy with her cousin.

The road was along the Grand River. As they drove along they saw an object standing on the river bank at a place they knew was clear of trees and shrubs. It seemed just to have come out of the water.

The moon was bright and their road wound to within three feet of the object so they knew they would get a clearer view when they got closer. When they got quite near, they could see it was the figure of a man, standing in the moonlight. He was in soldier's uniform and he was very tall, but as the shadow shifted they saw he had no head. There was an object the size of a head on the ground beside the man.

When he heard this story, an old man in the neighborhood predicted that something would happen involving soldiers. And indeed his prediction was right: that was the year the First World War was declared.

Tutela Heights
Tutela Heights is on the banks of the Grand River near Brantford. It was once an Indian settlement, owned by the Tutela tribe, but the Tutelas were wiped out by the whites in a bloody battle. Now they say the Tutelas come back every twenty years to avenge the slaughter.

In a year when their return was expected, two Mohawk women were picnicking on the road to the heights, at noon. They began to hear tom-toms, and then war cries and while they sat there, the sound got closer and closer till it was almost upon them. They fled.

During the same year a Mohawk with his uncle and a neighbor were walking home to the reserve from Brantford. It was a still, moonlit night, and the three men sat down on

the river bank to rest and smoke a pipe. First they heard a noise as though someone were splashing in the river. Then they heard the tom-toms and war cries, which approached, passed the spot where they were sitting and faded into the distance beyond. There was nothing to be seen.

The headless passenger

This happened to the boy who lived on the next farm and his mother. It was in the spring of the year.

The night was dark and it was raining very hard when the woman and her son started for home. They had been with her daughter, the boy's sister, all day. She was ill with an incurable disease. They were driving a team of horses hitched to a wagon. The ditches on each side of the road were filled with water. Because of the storm, the oil lantern would not stay lit, so they had to wait for the lightning flashes to see the road. The thunder was almost continuous.

When they were about half way home, tense with peering so they would not miss the bridge on the road, the mother suddenly muttered to her son that she thought someone had climbed into the back of the wagon. He couldn't spare a glance just then, but at the next lightning flash he looked to see who it was. It was a man sitting in the back of the wagon with his coat over his head. The son called 'Sago', which means 'Hello', for he was glad of company on such a night. The man did not answer. At the next flash of lightning the boy and his mother both looked, and it was then that they saw the passenger had no head. At that moment the horses screamed and broke into a gallop along a road where the houses were spaced far apart. The boy and his mother did not see when the headless man got out, but when the horses quieted down they looked back and he was gone.

Many people have seen this man, and the story is that someone had been killed on that road. He has never hurt anyone, but he has frightened many. Sometimes he has been seen riding a bicycle.

The gambler

There was a man on the reserve who lived only for gambling, though he was the son of a preacher. But the time came when he stopped gambling entirely and didn't go out at night and never went near his old haunt, which was a community hall where the boys gathered for a good time. At weekends they sometimes stayed there all night.

An old man asked the gambler what had happened to make him change his ways so completely and this is the story he finally told.

He was walking home from a night of gambling and drinking, so drunk he could scarcely stagger. A well-dressed man came towards him down the road and when they stood face-to-face the man challenged the gambler to a game of cards, the sky's the limit. The gambler said at once, 'Where shall we play?' The stranger answered, 'Right here and now.' The gambler brought out his pack of cards and his money and they squatted in the road to play. The gambler lost heavily and when most of his money was gone he said he had better go home. The stranger laid a hand on his arm and said, 'Not so fast. You and I have not finished our game.' The stranger's touch burned the arm, and the gambler, suddenly sober, said his money was gone and he was not going to stay. When he straightened up the stranger had vanished. His cards were in his pocket and the stranger's winnings were heaped by the side of the road.

The gambler was alone. Yet as he took off for home, he felt someone was following him. The footsteps behind him grew louder and he broke into a run. His back felt cold and a hissing noise was growing in his head and he seemed to hear chains rattling. He tried to remember some of his father's prayers. Then he thought of his mother, and of his brother who would be safe asleep in the room they shared. With his pursuer almost at his back he reached the house, flung open the door and took the stairs two at a time, pausing at the top only to pull out his deck of cards and throw it down the stairs. He could hear the cards land and scatter.

77

When he got to his bed he woke his brother and told him what had happened. It was already daybreak and his brother waited while he changed into work clothes. As they started going downstairs together, the gambler found that the cards he had scattered were neatly stacked on the top landing. He picked them up, took them downstairs, and in front of his father and mother and brother threw them into the kitchen stove.

Later he and his brother went to the place where the game had been played. The pile of wood chips was still there. Beside it, in another pile, was the money he had lost to the stranger.

Sulphur and chains

Forbidden Voice's mother often told this story. The couple had once lived on the next farm.

Winter was just about over. The warming rays of the sun were melting the snow and ice, and water lay about everywhere. It made it difficult to get from place to place.

One night a man and his wife were invited to a dance three miles away. They had no means of transport, and the weather had turned to freezing rain, but the wife wanted to go and begged and begged her husband. He told her there would be other parties when the weather was nicer, and she became angry. She said she would go without him. She said even the devil himself could not make her stay at home.

Off she went. The husband went to bed but he could not sleep. The rain was coming down now in torrents. He looked at his watch. She had been gone for six hours. She would be having a fine time at the dance by now.

Suddenly the front door burst open and his wife fell in a heap on the floor. When he went to her, her eyes were wild with fright and she could not speak. She kept staring back at the door. She was cold, her whole body trembled and beads of sweat stood out on her forehead. Her husband helped her to bed and when she could speak a little she begged him to stay by her side till first light and then she would tell him what had happened.

At daybreak this is what she told him. When

she had left the house to go to the dance, she had avoided the standing water as much as she could, climbing fences and taking short cuts through the fields. By the time she reached the main road she was soaked through. It was pitch dark, but she was still determined to get to the dance so she plodded on and on. After a while it seemed to her that there was something even darker than the night keeping just ahead of her. Then she got to a bridge, and just as she set foot on it the darkness gathered into a looming shape that closed in on her and began to smother her. She tried to dodge aside, but it moved with her. She beat at it, but her hands felt nothing. The darkness was into her throat and choking her and she knew she was going to faint. Everything went black for a moment and through the blackness she smelt sulphur and heard the rattle of chains. After a second she turned and ran, but no matter how fast she ran she could still smell the sulphur and hear the chains.

She ran through ditches filled with water, and kept falling to her knees. She lost her way again and again. Even as she saw the lamplight in the window of her house and stumbled in the door, she could hear the chains.

This woman developed pneumonia and died in two weeks. Now the house where she and her husband lived stands deserted. Sometimes hunters enter it to rest or to get in out of a storm.

Cats

There was a family on the reserve, a young man, his wife and two small children, who lived in a two-roomed shack back in the woods. Late one stormy night in January, well past midnight, the mother was baking pies when there was a loud knock at the door. She opened it and recognized the ten-year-old grandson of an old woman who lived half a mile away. She brought him in and brushed the snow from his clothes, and all the while he was telling her that his grandmother had sent him to borrow some flour. He said that they had had nothing to eat for two days but that his grandmother would go to the store the next day and

then she would return the flour. The mother gave him the flour, and he left the house about two o'clock in the morning.

There had been something strange about the boy and that night the mother dreamed about him. She dreamed that the boy and his grandmother had turned into two huge cats, and that there were no windows or doors in their house.

The next morning, the mother was still worried, and got her husband to stay with the children while she went to see if everything was all right with the boy and his grandmother. There was no track to follow and the snow was very deep and as she passed a neighboring house she stopped and asked the neighbor to keep her company.

When they got to the old lady's house, her daughter let them in. She said she was glad to see them, for her mother had been dead for two days, and the grandson had been sent away to stay with friends. The daughter took them into another room and there was the old woman laid out on boards, wearing a bright yellow dress and a long string of yellow beads and a watch.

Then the daughter told them that in her last moments the old woman had kept seeing cats. They were everywhere—on her ceiling, on the walls, on her bed. She was frightened and screamed so much that she fell out of bed.

While the three women stood talking beside the body, the old woman's face began to twitch. Her eyelids struggled to open and her mouth stretched into distorted shapes. The mother and her neighbor fled and one of them sent word to a minister asking him to go and see the dead woman.

When he came and saw her he ordered the coffin closed and it was not opened again.

The hanged man

An Indian was accused of a murder he had not committed. The man who could have saved him was so afraid of getting involved that he fell ill, too ill to testify. So now an innocent man was being hanged.

His wife had left him before this, and was

living in a house by herself when he was brought to trial, and sentenced and hanged. They buried the man the same day he was hanged.

That night his wife dreamed he came to the house where she was living. She heard him in the road calling her name in rage, and she recognized his footstep outside the door. In her dream she was terrified, and locked the door and ran upstairs. Downstairs she could hear him pounding on the door and calling for her to open it. She kept very still. Then she heard a splintering noise and knew the pounding had burst open the wooden door. She ran to the window and screamed for her neighbors and as she screamed she woke up.

The next morning she came downstairs to find the front door in splinters.

CODES AND CEREMONIES OF THE CONFEDERACY

Forbidden Voice learns her duties
The League of Peace
The code of the chiefs

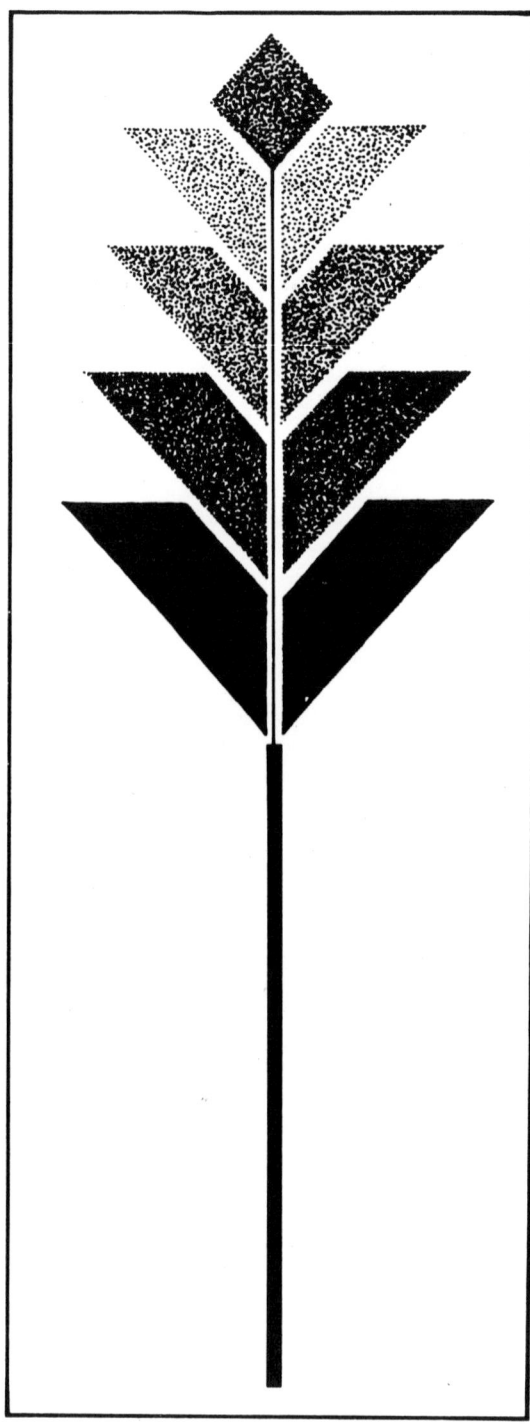

One day Forbidden Voice's mother told her to come with her. They hurried together to the house of their chief—the chief of the Turtle Clan—and up to his bedroom. There they saw all the other chiefs gathered together in ceremonial dress. Their own chief was in his bed, lying wasted and sick, with his eyes closed. The other chiefs placed a chair in the centre of the room for her mother and another chair for little Forbidden Voice, who had been given her mother's wampum beads to carry.

Then a ceremony began. First one chief walked back and forth, then he went up to the sick man and bowed and said in Mohawk, 'Now I take the horns'. Then he held up his hands as though he were carrying something, crossed to the wall, and went through the motions of hanging up something, though he really didn't have anything in his hands. Afterwards all the chiefs in turn did the same. Then a string of black wampum was hung by the bed and the ceremony was over.

This was the first time Forbidden Voice was present at a sacred clan rite. Her mother had already explained that the 'horns' were the deer's antlers that the Great Spirit had placed upon the heads of all ordained chiefs as emblems of power. There did not actually need to be real horns, for the ceremony, a symbolic taking away of the chief's authority, was enough.

Now her mother explained that the form of the ceremony was incorporated in the constitution of the confederacy, handed down for many generations, where it said: 'If a lord becomes ill, the lords of the confederacy shall visit the dying lord and take his deer's horns off his head and place them beside the wall so that if by the will of the Great Spirit he recovers from his illness, he will resume the crown of deer's horns and resume the duties of a lord. During his illness, a string of black wampum is hung at the head of his bed. If he dies, anyone belonging to his clan will take this string of black wampum and announce his death to the whole circle of the confederacy. In case of sudden death of a lord, his colleagues, the chiefs, will remove his crown of deer's horns

and the chief matron will place them on his successor's head'.

This first ceremony marked the real beginning of the little girl's training as a princess and possible clan mother. Her father began taking her to political meetings, and many times they journeyed to New York State, or to the Oneida Reservation near London, Ontario. She began to learn that things had been done to the Indians by white governments and many laws passed about them without consulting the Indians or getting their consent.

She was taken to other Indian ceremonies. Once she went with her father when the chiefs of the confederacy gathered at the home of Chief Blind Gibson, after he was dead, to take off the horns of authority so they would be ready for his clan mother to confer on his successor. The little girl saw Chief Gibson in the coffin in his ceremonial Indian costume and she also saw the lunch that had been prepared and placed inside the coffin to sustain him on the heaven-road.

She went several times when new chiefs were ordained. This was a long ceremony that started in the morning and lasted all day and the best part of the night. Sometimes she was given a chair in their midst, but mostly she stood to take part like the men. When other tribes received the chiefs of the confederacy, she went with them and stood at the front and shook hands just like them. She never saw another child at these ceremonies but she was a princess of the eternal clan and of the tribe of leaders.

Meanwhile her mother had also begun to teach her the lore and code of the confederacy, which were transmitted from one generation to the next by word of mouth, by certain hieroglyphic records cut or painted on staves of wood or on strips of skin, and by the wampum belts.

In this code it was recorded that Dehganawihdeh was the founder of the League of Peace, and Hiawatha, one of the five ordained chiefs, was his spokesman. The woman Jikonsaseh was the direct descendant of the first woman born on earth, and her line was the blood line of the official seal, recognized by all the tribes that were Onweh (redskins). The descent of blood was traced in the female line. From this came the right of women of the confederacy to nominate or even depose the lords of the confederacy.

In this code it was also recorded that peace was the law of the land, and the symbol of peace was the Tree of Peace, which Dehganawihdeh had planted. The branches of the tree signified shelter, protection and security. The roots which stretched to the four corners of the earth signified the extension of the law. People who desired peace would follow the roots to their source and take shelter under the tree. The eagle which Dehganawihdeh placed on top of the tree signified watchfulness.

It was recorded that the confederacy should be ruled by a council of the hereditary chiefs and that the three 'elder' tribes, the Mohawks, the Senecas and the Onondagas, should have special roles. Thus the Mohawks were the sponsors of new ideas, the Senecas were 'the keepers of the western door', and the Onondagas were the firekeepers and the custodians of the wampum.

It was recorded that after Dehganawihdeh had set up the confederacy and ordained the hereditary chiefs, the chiefs formed their first council fire. The white wampum beads were the emblem of the law, and the Onondaga lord, who was the firekeeper, held this string of wampum in his hand when he opened the council by offering thanksgiving to the Great Spirit. When the council was in session the string of wampum was placed in their midst, and the pipe of peace was smoked. At the close of the council, the Onondaga chief picked up the wampum, held it in his hand and again offered thanksgiving. So it was to be done for all time.

It was also recorded that the chiefs themselves should be governed by a code, and this was the code:

If a lord is found guilty of willful murder, he shall be deposed without warning by the lords of the confederacy and his horns shall be

handed back to the chief matron of his family and clan.

If a lord is guilty of rape, he shall be deposed without warning and his horns shall be handed back to the chief matron of his family and clan.

If a lord is guilty of theft he is to be deposed.

If a lord is guilty of unwarrantedly opposing the decisions of his brother lords, or of showing disrespect for them, he shall be approached by the chief matron of his family and clan to urge him to desist from his evil practices. If the lord still refuses to listen and obey, a warrior of his clan will approach him to desist from his ways. If the lord still refuses to obey, the chief warrior shall take the deer's horns from his head and give them back to the chief matron. Then the matron will select and appoint another warrior of her family and crown him. A new lord is created in the place of the one deposed.

When a lord is deposed and the emblem of power is taken from him, he shall not be allowed to sit in council or hold an office again. If a lord is deceased, the chief matron and the warriors of the family clan will nominate another warrior of the same clan to succeed the deceased. If the family and clan in which a lordship is vested become extinct, the confederate council will consider the matter, and nominate and appoint a successor from any family of the brother lords of the deceased.

Here, as part of this code, was where it was also laid down what was to happen if a lord became ill, or if he died suddenly, which were the ceremonies Forbidden Voice had already seen.

But there was a great deal more for Forbidden Voice to learn. She was taught that, as a princess and a future clan mother, she had a sacred obligation to keep the blood line pure and must marry, when the time came, someone from her own clan. She was also taught about morality. Her father, who was a reserved man with a gentle face, talked to her about anger, reminding her that Mohawks did not get angry and that there was not even a curse-word in their language. He said that if you didn't add more sticks to a fire you could watch it go out, and if you didn't add anger to a quarrel, it too would die. 'Don't add another stick to the fire', he said.

Her mother, who had black hair parted in the centre, and a slim, stern face, taught her that good behavior was more than being afraid of the Hand or the Naked Leg. She must never touch alcohol, and never take up with a white man, and she must keep a thankful heart for all the Great Spirit's blessings.

HANDSOME LAKE

A Seneca prophet of the
eighteenth century

It was her mother who told her the story of Handsome Lake and the dream of Handsome Lake.

Handsome Lake was a real man. He had been a Seneca prophet and when he was well past middle age he had a dream and embarked on a sacred mission exhorting all Indians to forsake the ways of the white man and return to the ancient paths of the tribal religion. He preached temperance and morality.

Handsome Lake was a half brother to Corn Planter, the Seneca sachem, and for many years in his youth he lived the life of a drunkard. All the same, he was aware of the greedy eyes of the foreign enemy as he saw the lands of his forefathers dwindle for the sake of a swig of trader's rum.

Here is how he came to change his ways. Handsome Lake fell very ill. For four years he lay in bed and all that time there grew in him a feeling that he must get well, for he had a mission to fulfil. One day a feeling of happiness swelled in him and he felt well enough to rise from his bed. When he got outside, his daughter saw him and came running, but when she got to him, Handsome Lake fell into her arms and she thought he was dead. Others came and carried him into the house and dressed him for burial. His nephew and his other daughter were sent for, with the message that he had lain so long in bed he was dead. Everyone hearing of the death of a man goes to where he lies. When the nephew came he touched the dead man on every part of his body. When he felt the chest there was a warm spot and he told the people the man might yet revive.

At noon of the next day Handsome Lake opened his eyes. His lips moved as if to speak, though no words came forth. At length he said, 'Yes, I believe myself well. Never have I seen such wondrous visions.'

He told them that he had heard a voice say thrice, 'Come out a while'. Because he was ill he had thought it was his own voice, but when it came again he rose from his bed and went outside. There, in the clear swept space, he saw three men dressed in white. Their cheeks were

painted red, though it seemed they had been painted the day before. The three beings looked alike, and were middle-aged, and each carried a bow and arrow in one hand and in the other huckleberry bushes with berries of every color.

The three beings spoke and said, 'He who created the world at the beginning employed us to come to earth. Our visit now is not the only one we have made.' They told Handsome Lake to eat huckleberries of each color. Then they said that the following morning they would have a fire in the bushes and medicine steeped to give him strength. Meanwhile, they said, the people must gather at the council house to celebrate his recovery with a strawberry feast and all must drink the strawberry juice in humble thanksgiving.

So it was done. Then Handsome Lake gathered all the records of his evil life and placed them before the throne of mercy and said he was ready.

First the three beings told him to look through the valley between two hills, and to look between the sunrise and the noon, and as he looked he saw a deep gap in the valley from which came smoke and steam. The three beings said a man was buried in the hole, and with him a great message they had once commanded him to proclaim to all the world, but because the man had disobeyed, he would never rise from that spot. Now they were going to give the same message to Handsome Lake, charging him to carry it truthfully to all people.

They said: 'The Creator is sad, for four words have brought great trouble to his people. The first word is Onega (firewater). It is a monstrous evil and has raised a high mound of human bones. When the people hear this message they must stop the evil. The Creator made Onega to be used as medicine.

'The second word is Yagotgonh (witch). Witches are without right minds. They make diseases and spread sickness to make the living die; they cut short the numbered days the Creator has given each person. When the

witches hear this message, they must confess before all the people and the Creator.

'The third word is a sad one. It is the word for the secret poison in little bundles, the compelling charms. Under the compelling charms people are brought to deceit, immorality and murder. Let everyone hear this message and repent for fear the Creator will not accept them as his own.

'The fourth word is abortion. The female man-beings were created to bear children and one must never administer medicine to prevent children from coming.

'There is also a severe punishment for the married man who leaves two women with a child; and a greater punishment for the man who leaves the third. The same punishment awaits the female man-being who complies in his sins.

'When a man returns home in drink he must not touch or fondle his little child. If he does, he will burn the child's blood.

'No one must speak evil of little children;

whosoever does right to the aged, does right in the eyes of the Creator.

'The Creator made food for all creatures. When visitors enter your lodge you must offer them food to eat; whosoever feeds the poor does right in the eyes of the Creator.

'No one shall call a dance in honour of some totem animal from which he desires favor or power; those who belong to totem animal societies must throw the sacred tobacco and disband.

'It has been ordered that at certain times there should be thanksgiving ceremonies. At that time all must thank the Creator for life.

'It is a prophecy that the white serpent will exterminate the people, but there is nothing to fear. The Creator will care for His people.'

After this, Handsome Lake was told about the coming of the end of the earth. When the end is near, the chiefs and head men will disagree and that will be a sign; and the earth will withhold its sustaining foods and that will be a sign. The witch will perform her witch spells

in the daylight. She will run through the neighborhood calling out the number of those she has killed. Every poisonous creature will appear: they are the creatures of the evil spirit that the Creator imprisoned in the underworld. But now they will be released and will poison many.

At the end the faithful will enter a deep sleep in perfect health and while they sleep the Creator will withdraw their lives. But a great plague will kill many of the unbelievers. And when the end comes the earth will be destroyed by fire; not one person will escape who does not believe in the great Creator.

Next the three beings revealed to Handsome Lake the House of the Punished and the Lands of the Creator. Suddenly a road descended from the south sky and came to where they were standing, and this is what Handsome Lake saw when he walked along the road.

There was a strongly built house and in it were a pair of handcuffs, a whip and a hangman's rope. This house was the prison, but no one need enter this house if he believes and accepts the Creator's message. Then Handsome Lake saw a large woman sitting and snatching at everything within reach until she was so weighed down she could not stand up. He was told that what he saw was the sin of stinginess, and of those who forsake religion; they cannot stand on the heaven-road.

Beyond, Handsome Lake saw two roads. One was narrow, where little children walked, and the other was wide. He saw a woman take the narrow road. Earth people knew her to have a dark and sinful past but a voice said that she had repented, and because of her sincerity she had been led to the narrow road that leads to the lands of the Creator.

The three beings and Handsome Lake took the wide rough road that leads to the lodge of the Punisher; and as they walked towards it they felt heat coming from the house and heard the cries of the doomed. Within the building hot vapor was rising from fire pits, and a being with cloven hoofs walked about as if he were master. He was the Punisher. The Punisher held a glass of molten metal to the lips of a

drunkard and compelled him to drink. The drunkard screamed with a loud voice and fell to the ground with vapors streaming from his throat.

The Punisher called out a woman's name, and when she appeared he forced her body into a cauldron filled with boiling liquid. She came to the surface crying out like some strange animal, and then sank again, and each time she came to the surface the scream was louder. This was the punishment for those who practice witchcraft. The witch will suffer two deaths, for when her body is reduced to dust, the Punisher will gather it up and conjure it back into a living body until at length he will blow her ashes to destruction.

Now the Punisher called a man and showed him an image of a woman heated with fire and told him to flog his wife as he had on earth. The man struck the fiery image with his bare hands, and fell to the floor in agony. This was the punishment for a man who beats his wife.

After this Handsome Lake and the three beings went on the narrow road, and saw at a distance a light more radiant than any he had ever seen. Handsome Lake smelled the perfume of flowers growing along the way. There were delicious fruits, and every kind of bird flew in the air above them. All these things were on the heaven-road.

After his vision Handsome Lake became the founder of a new religious system. He taught his followers that the clothes they wore, the houses they lived in and the longhouses they worshipped in might be made of white man's material, but that was just the surface. Their religion was not of paint or feathers but of the heart.

When Handsome Lake preached his message of good tidings at Cold Spring Village, there was a certain man who stood in the doorway showing disgust and disrespect. At the end of the meeting this man did not make his way home. The next day he was still missing and the people organised a search party. Two days later they found him in a swamp. He had formed a nest of broken branches and he sat in it eating snakes. They took the poor man from his nest back to his own home where he died soon after.

Handsome Lake was born on the Genesee Reserve in New York State in 1735 and, after his vision, spent the rest of his life preaching to the Indians to return to the true tribal worship of the Creator. He died on August 10, 1815, and was buried at the Onondaga longhouse on the Onondaga Reserve.

It was during his lifetime that Captain Joseph Brant destroyed the Mohawk longhouse for the sake of Christianity.

DREAMS

A vision of the afterlife
Dreams as omens and portents

Indians believe that dreams have meaning.

When Forbidden Voice was eleven, her mother became very ill with pneumonia. It was the night of the sixth of January. The family had gone to a Twelfth Night party on the reserve. Forbidden Voice was still full of excitement because there had been a tree with gifts, and a play about Hiawatha, written by the minister's daughter, and she had had a part in the play. On the way home her father had tucked her in a blanket and put her in a clothes basket tied to a hand sleigh and pulled her home through the bright night with starlight frosting the snowy trees. When they got home her father had started a fire in the heater and everyone stood around for a while in their wraps until the room was cosy.

Then, about three in the morning, her mother fell ill. The doctor came in the morning, and every day after that for fourteen days. Then there came a terrible three days when her mother slipped into a coma and the doctor told them to give up hope. When the family left her mother's room at meal times, Forbidden Voice would stay there by herself and pray to the Great Spirit to spare her. On the morning of the fourth day of her mother's coma, Forbidden Voice's father came and roused her and told her to come quickly for her mother was dying. When someone in a family dies, everyone must come–no one must be left sleeping. So Forbidden Voice left her bed and rushed to her mother's bedside screaming 'Mother, don't leave me'. Her mother slowly opened her eyes and smiled. 'No I will not leave you', she said. 'Not for a little while.'

Presently she began to talk. She said she had been a long way away, and after she had walked a distance, she had reached the River of Life. Over the water towards her came a girl, holding out her hand and saying, 'Mother I have come to meet you.' It was Josephine, the daughter who had died when she was sixteen, before Forbidden Voice was born. Josephine told her mother not to be afraid, and hand in hand they walked through the water. When they reached the other side, the mother found her clothes were as white as snow and there

was great peace in her soul. As they walked on, she saw the houses that mortals prepare for themselves in the hereafter. One she described was a house made of roses – for each good deed on earth a rose had been added. The air was fragrant with their perfume, and each rose was a beacon of light illuminating the house with rainbow colours. Then the mother asked to see her other precious babies, who had died in their infancy. It was then that Josephine said to her, 'I cannot take you further. You will have to go back, for the prayers of my youngest sister, asking that you be spared, have been heard in heaven. You must go back for her sake.'

The mother turned back. She saw a crowd at a distance and as she drew nearer, she saw it was a funeral procession. It was her coffin, and two maidens were walking behind it dressed in deep mourning with black veils almost covering their faces. When they turned, she saw they were her two living daughters and then she knew she would live until her daughters were grown women.

A man approached and told her she would come presently to a flock of sheep and one would have a light blue ribbon round its neck. If she could catch this one, she would be allowed to stay, but if she could not she would have to return to earth. She walked on and there were the sheep, the one with the blue ribbon standing apart from the rest. She tried to catch it but could not keep her grip, so she walked on.

Then she met the man who had approached her before, and he told her that when she reached her home a seamstress would be there with her gown. If the gown fit properly she could return with the seamstress. The seamstress was there when she reached home and in her hand was a beautiful shimmering blue gown. But when she put it on, the gown had only one sleeve, and so she went to her bedroom and there were her family around her bed. She heard Forbidden Voice's despairing cry, 'Mother, don't leave me'.

Forbidden Voice was very struck by this dream of her mother's, and became interested

in all dreams and began collecting them. At school she asked her schoolmates what they had dreamt about, and sometimes she asked the men who came to the house and other people she met. She found that everyone was eager to talk about his dreams, and to argue about what they meant; for her people believed there was always a meaning, if only it could be understood. Sometimes the meaning was easy to see and sometimes it was very hard.

The swamp

A twelve-year-old boy had a raging temperature. He had been to school all day and afterwards he had played with his friends in the swamp. When he came home his clothes were wet, and his mother sent him to bed.

During the night he had this dream. He was back in the swamp with his friends, playing the same game they had played that afternoon. All of a sudden the swamp cracked open and his friends slid one by one into the gap. He saved himself by grabbing the branch of a dead tree, but he knew it wouldn't be long before he too fell in. The swamp trembled and shook, and he could hear his playmates screaming for help. Then he saw strange animals swarming into the crevasse, glaring up at him hungrily. His arms ached and were just about to give way when he heard a roaring behind him. He turned to see a lion poised to attack.

The lion said to the boy, 'Have no fear. I will help you. I am the king of the jungle and I give all the commands.' The lion roared again. All the animals saluted him and one by one went back into the gap. As they went they tossed back the school friends to the surface again.

A mad bull

A little girl was awakened by her mother one night: she had been screaming at the top of her lungs.

She had dreamed that she was at school playing with the boys and girls as usual. Only this time one of the boys came running to tell them that a mad bull had escaped. It was coming down the road towards them. All the

107

other children ran to hide, but this girl found she couldn't move. She managed to get as far as the school house and went inside and crouched beneath the window. But the bull was right behind her and it raised the window and started to crawl through. She screamed and screamed, pleading with the bull to chase the other boys and girls instead, calling out their names. The bull nodded his head and ran the other way and the little girl woke up.

Bogeyman

The little boy was only five but he wouldn't listen when his mother told him he mustn't eat so much just before he went to bed. Finally she told him that if he didn't obey he would see 'the bogeyman' when he went to sleep.

Sometime during the night she was wakened by his screams. After she had gone and quieted him he said, 'I saw it. You told me I would see it'. When she asked him what he saw, he said, 'the bogeyman'. He said it was just the head of a horse floating in the water. Its eyes were blinking and it was looking at him.

The Dance

Two teen-age girls had been trying to coax their parents into letting them go to the dances at the community hall. But their parents were unwilling.

One night one of them had a dream. She had arrived at a party, the music was playing and most of her friends were there. A pleasant-looking boy asked her to dance. While they were dancing the girl suddenly realised that the violinist had turned into a slender black rat. The man who was 'calling' off was now an overgrown frog: and every time he spoke his lips quacked, so that it sounded like people clapping. When the girl looked at her own partner, he had changed into a grasshopper. Every time they swung around he hopped and hopped, taking her with him. Then he jumped so hard that they both fell down, and she woke up as she came down with a thud in her own bed.

The girl friend

A teen-age girl dreamed that her mother gave a party for her, to which all her girl friends were invited.

When the time came, there was a big cake on the table with the names of her friends inscribed in gold. They were all having a good time playing games when someone knocked at the door. It was a strange man who said he had come to warn them that one of the girls who had not yet arrived had become mentally unbalanced. She was supposed to be at home, but she had got away from her parents and was on her way.

Before he could say any more, someone grabbed him from behind and threw him to the floor and ran past him into the room. It was the 'unhinged' girl, and she was looking for the girl whose party it was because she meant to do her harm. The girl dreamed she was in terror and couldn't get away, until suddenly she discovered she could fly. She flew from one room to another with her pursuer still behind her. But then she was able to get out the door and she flew away over the tree tops.

The snake

A little boy dreamed that a snake as big as a seven-inch pipe was going after a little girl who was his cousin. The boy yelled at her to run home, but the snake chased right behind her, through fields and over fences, spitting fire as it went.

Just as the little girl reached her home, the boy managed to climb on the snake's back, and was pounding it with his fists when the snake looked back at him. It had the face of a beautiful man, and it spoke. 'Why do you do that? I brought gifts for the little girl for her birthday.'

A basket of gold

An old couple had lived in poverty all their lives. Now they had hardly enough to eat. One cold night the husband went out in search of food and the wife, who was feeling cold and sick, went to bed. When she finally got warm enough she went to sleep and had a dream.

She dreamed someone told her that her husband had lost his way in the snow and had been found lying along the old snake fence, frozen to death. She was trying to get out of bed when she heard a knock at the door. A man entered carrying a basket of apples which he placed on the table. They were so bright they dazzled her eyes. She asked him where he had found such lovely applies. He said, 'They only look like apples – they are solid gold.'

While the old woman was dreaming, her husband had come home, and when he heard her mumbling he came to her. She told him about her dream. She said she would rather have him alive than apples made of gold.

Greed

A widow was about to have her mortgage foreclosed. She could hardly sleep for worry, but one night when she did fall asleep from sheer exhaustion she dreamed she was in a strange town, looking for a place to stay.

When she stopped to enquire, a storekeeper told her of a house, only a mile away, that might be for sale at a reasonable sum. He had the key, and if she wanted to see it she could go and spend the night there.

To her surprise it was a lovely little house, well furnished. She chose one of the bedrooms to sleep in, at the opposite end of the hall to a room marked Store Room.

The widow went to bed and was awakened during the night by groans. But none of the lights would work so she stayed in her room. At daylight the groans could still be heard, and she followed the sound to the Store Room. Inside she found the skeleton of a woman, clutching a bundle of money. The skeleton began to talk. 'Do not be afraid', it said. 'I was once a landlady who showed no mercy and had no pity. Now I must stay here like this among my bundles of money. You may stay here as long as you like. It may help me to atone.'

Warts

Two high-spirited men in the community were always getting into mischief. They were not bad men, but they were thoughtless and reckless to the point that they had even got mixed up with the law. Their friends started turning away from them.

One woman who liked the men and worried about their families had a dream one night. She dreamed the two men were in her back yard talking to her two brothers. A well-dressed man approached them, and when he got close enough they could see he had horns and cloven feet.

The woman went out of the house to them, and she saw at once that the two men had grown ugly warts on their faces and arms. They looked frightened and helpless. The woman knew what to do. She walked to the two men and held their hands towards heaven and prayed in a loud voice. One by one the warts disappeared. The horned visitor vanished.

The next day she made a point of telling the two men about her dream, and after that they seemed to change.

Repentance

A girl from a respectable family grew restless in the country and left for the bright city lights. She had been gone for twelve years when suddenly she reappeared in her old home, even though her parents were long since dead.

This is the story she told a friend. For a long while she had led a gay life in the city. She tossed letters from home unopened into her trunk. Though from time to time her mother's lessons returned to haunt her, she kept on with wild nights and wild parties until just three weeks before her return. Then she had had a dream about the life she was leading which was so horrible she didn't want to talk about it and did her best to forget it. She went on as before.

Then, after three weeks, she had another dream. In this one she saw two roads. One was the road to destruction and on it she saw herself and her friends in a wild dance. But it was not a dance for fun. They were being lashed as they went along the road, and they were being forced to drink from bottles containing molten lead. Then she saw the face of her mother. It

113

was so full of sadness that the girl cried for mercy and help. At that moment she seemed to hear a voice say, 'Repent now. This is your last chance'.

Though both her parents were long since dead, she packed her trunk the next day and came home.

The Saviour
This is the dream of an old chief. In it he saw the people of his tribe in great distress. They were being driven into a swamp with guns and bayonets. The water was red with blood and he could hear the screams of the children. While he was pondering how to save them, he went around to the back of his house. There, under the shade of his maple tree, were two long benches. Men of every nation had gathered, and they were in general discussion. Then one man stood up and said, 'I will save these people.'

The old chief swears he will recognize this man if he should ever see him.

Vision
A young man who was dying of an incurable disease told a friend he had had a dream that puzzled him. This was in horse-and-buggy days.

In his dream he was outside his home and he could hear a noise like the distant rumble of thunder along the road. It came closer and then he saw a buggy go past like lightning, with nothing to push or pull it.

After it had passed, he heard the same sort of thunder, but in the sky this time. He looked up and it was the same buggy, flying like a bird.

This young man died in 1911. He had never seen an automobile or an airplane.

Two graves
A woman dreamed she saw two men digging two graves in one cemetery, about four feet apart. As she watched, two ministers of two denominations approached. They had bitter words. One was asking the other why he had arranged his funeral service for the same time on the same day as his own. The second

minister finally said he would postpone his service until that night. Then he asked the woman if, in that case, she would take charge of the service since he had to attend an important meeting. It would keep him late but when he arrived he would sit with the mourners, and let her carry on. When the time came she was very nervous, but she picked out a hymn; and just before they started to sing she woke up.

The woman was still wondering what the dream meant when she fell asleep again and this time she was walking on the road in front of the same cemetery. There was a table that seemed to stretch for a mile and people were sitting on each side eating. She went closer and looked at the people. Those she knew were people who had been buried in the cemetery. Then she saw her own brother and went to him and asked him if there was a plate for her. He smiled and said no. She noticed that everyone was eating the same thing – a dark-colored porridge.

Daisies

In her dream she was a little girl again. Her grandfather had come to visit them and he was asleep on the lawn surrounded by daisies which had freshly bloomed that very morning. The little girl started picking the flowers and covering him with them like a blanket. She put them in his hair and even into the eyelets of his shoes. At that moment the grandfather opened his eyes and said, 'You are doing the same thing you did years ago, and you know what happened then.'

With that she remembered that she had done the same thing in real life, years ago, and that her grandfather had died soon after.

The wish

The man was very ill. He called his wife to sit by his bed while he told her a dream.

It seemed to him he had been away for a long time. Now he was back and wanted to see his family and the home where he had been happy with his wife and children, so he came home. He found the windows all boarded up and the place deserted.

115

He went round the house trying to peer inside, and when he got to the kitchen he found a little crack where he could look in. An old lady was sitting in a rocking-chair by the table, her face covered with her hands. She looked ragged and strange, and the room was peeling and strewn with crumbled plaster. Just then she took her hands away and he could see her face.

The man told his wife: 'It was you in the dream. I shall be leaving you soon. How I wish I could take you with me.'

The little old man

A mother had been nursing her tiny daughter for ten days. The baby had convulsions.

The mother finally fell asleep sitting by the bedside. She saw a little old man with a long beard walking around the bowl of her kerosene lamp on the night table. She watched him going around and around mumbling to himself. Finally he stopped and spoke to her.

He told her to go at once to the road. Her two grown sons had fought one another and now they were both lying dead at the edge of the swamp. She jumped up, lit the oil lantern and ran to the road calling their names. Though she walked up and down the edge of the swamp she couldn't find them. Finally, feeling the sting of the cold winter wind, she awoke.

It took her some time to realize she had been dreaming. When she did, just to make sure, she hurried to her sons' bedroom. They were safe and fast asleep. But her baby daughter was near the end.

Home alone

A little girl dreamed she was home alone late at night. She still had some homework to do and her books were upstairs. But just as she went to the stairs, she heard noises overhead. Then she remembered the old lady up there, who was very ill. Afraid to go up to her alone, she ran next door and got a school friend to go with her.

When they got back to the house, the queer noises were still going on so they went up together. When they got to the bedroom, they saw that the old lady had shed her skin like a snake, and the skin which had turned a yellowish green was lying on the bed. There was nothing else to be seen but a fox, running all over looking for a way to get out of the room. The skin kept saying, 'Help me but don't come near me.'

The luck charm

A young man from a very respected family wanted very badly to own a luck charm. A luck charm could be for good or evil, and every head householder had one. A luck charm was both a sentinel and a protector. It warned its owner of any threatening danger. In dire necessity it could go on missions for the owner—he had to burn the sacred tobacco and give it ritual instructions, and in ten days' time the luck charm would have performed the task. Luck charms were extra sensitive to threats from other luck charms. Luck charms throve on human blood, and had to be fed once a year.

The young man wanted one so badly that one night he had a dream. He dreamed he had been invited to the luck charms' annual convention along with all the other people who wanted to own one. He would be allowed to pick one he wanted, and it would stay in his family forever.

When he reached the meeting place, the convention was already in session. They gave him a place to sit so he could watch and listen and make up his mind which luck charm he wanted. The luck charms spoke one by one.

Finally a serpent rose to speak. He said, 'I have not had many man-beings pick me, for I am stern. If they disobey me, I will exterminate them. When I am summoned by my keeper, I serve him faithfully. But I can only be summoned near the edge of a large body of water because that is where I live.

'Sometimes when I answer the call, my keeper is so frightened he dies before I have finished his mission. I do not work alone. I have a master, the master of evil. He who selects me must sell his soul to my master. If he will, then he will find we can do anything we are asked to do, even destroy all the other luck-charms.'

The young man trembled. He knew what selling his soul to the devil meant. He would have to buy the luck-charm by killing the person he loved the most. He thought of his mother. He remembered how, when he was ill, her cool hands had soothed his aching body and how she had cried when his father died and he had comforted her, promising her his love and care forever. After he had killed his mother he would have to kill someone every year to pay the serpent's hire. He felt sick and trapped.

But the serpent was speaking again: 'Will someone escort the young man from this place. It is not the place for him. Go now and try to forget what you have seen.'

At that moment the young man awoke. He ran to find his mother and told her of his dream. When he had finished, she told him that she had known a family that had the serpent luck charm. The family was now extinct.

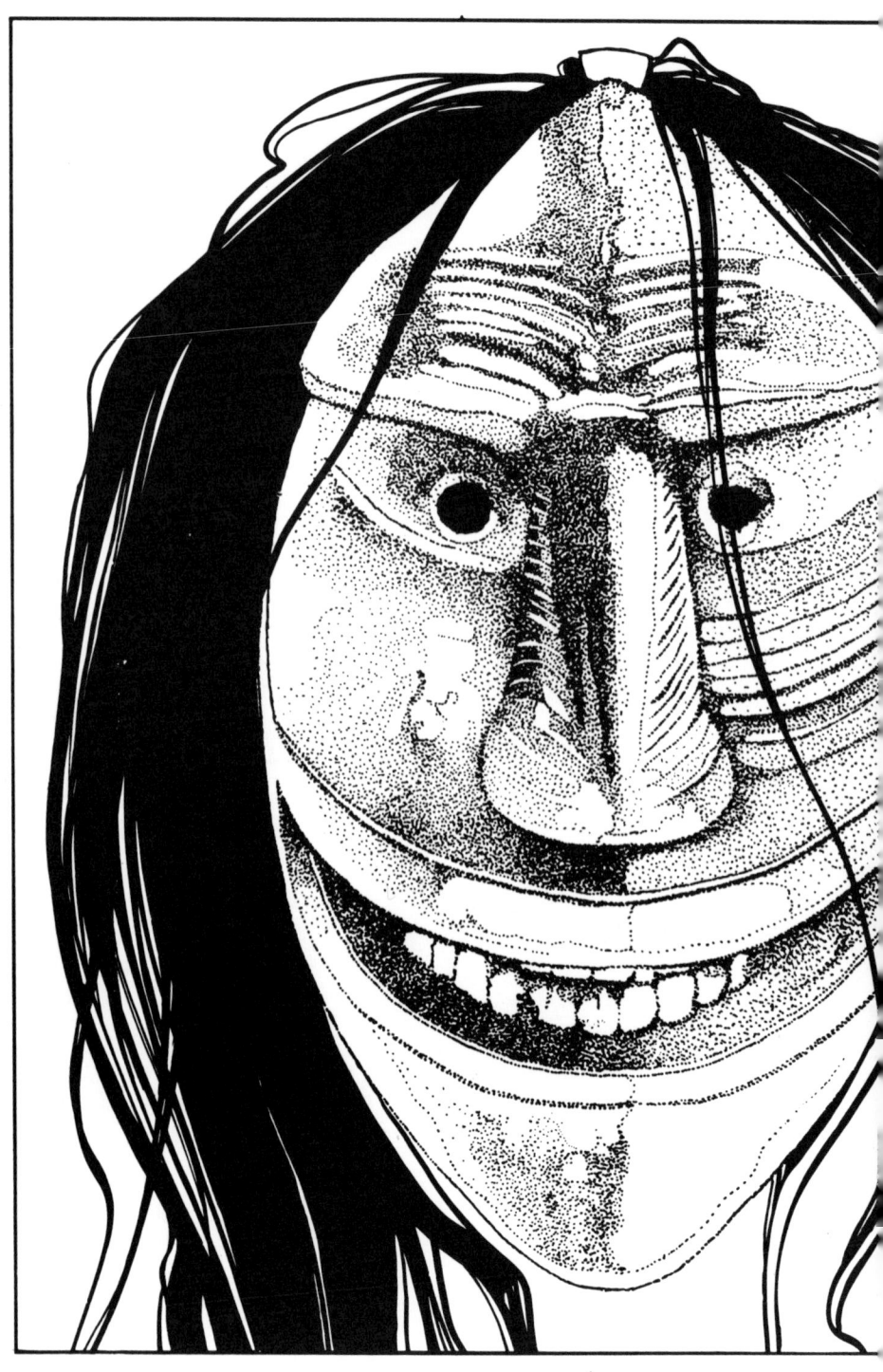

THE WHITE MAN'S WORLD

The New England Company
Christian missionaries
The Six Nations fight for England
A treaty dishonoured
Foreign customs in a
changing world

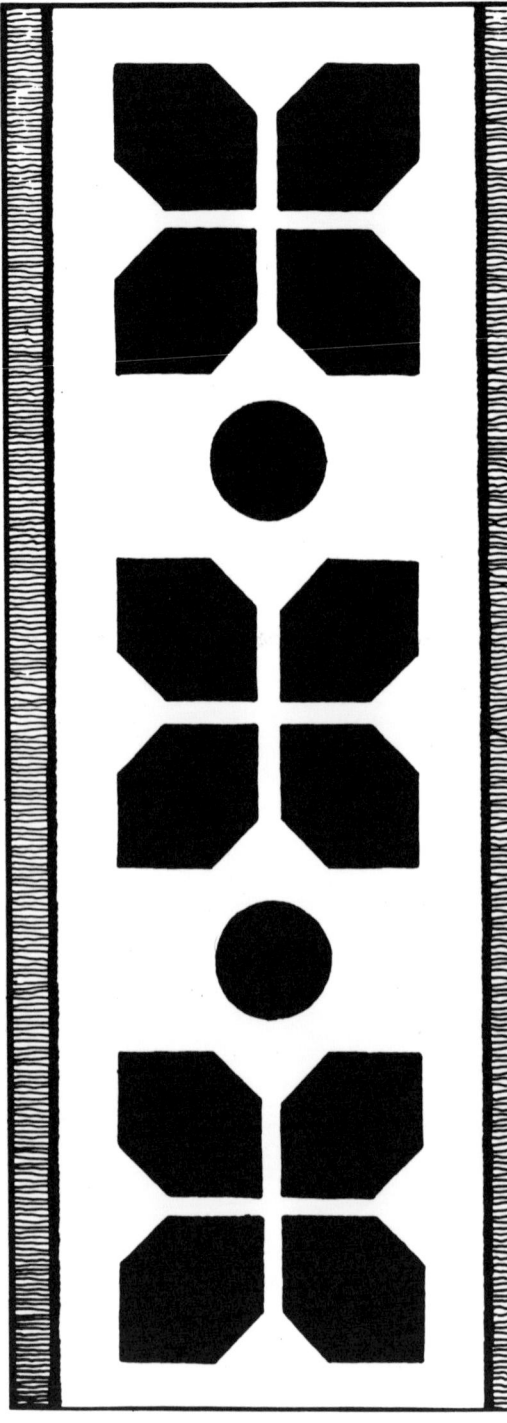

Everything was starting to change.

Both Forbidden Voice's big brothers were married now, and the older one had taken over the farm. The younger one had always preferred his paycheck to the life of a farmer, so his father had settled him in a house on a lot elsewhere on the reservation and the son went off to work every day. Forbidden Voice's big sister had gone to the city. People shook their heads when they talked about her.

Even Sundays were different now. Sunday had always been a special day in their house, Sunday was extra good meals, Sunday was put away all your work, even the doll's clothes you had been sewing. Sunday was visitors, Methodist church in the morning, and the Anglican church in the afternoon, and in the evening the whole family into the parlor for father to read from the Bible that sat on the fall-leaf table with the red cloth.

Her father was a lay reader in the Anglican church, and the first English Forbidden Voice had ever heard was her father reading the Bible on Sundays. For a long time the reading was just a monotone to her. She couldn't make out any of the words and the tiresome noise seemed to go on and on forever. It wasn't at all like the liquid Mohawk tongue, or even the jerky syllables of the Cayugas. Later, when she heard white men speak it, English was always to sound loud and quarrelsome in her ear.

Now her father had left the church and, though she asked him, he wouldn't say why. One day she mentioned this to an old chief who knew about affairs on the reserve, and he said he could tell her why. He took her to his house and there he showed her a document, which was a copy of the Exchequer Court proceedings between the Six Nations and the New England Company.

The New England Company was a curious organization that had been formed in the seventeenth century for the express purpose of 'civilizing' the North American natives and propagating the gospel. The company had sent missionaries to the Grand Valley in the 1820s and they had built a school for the Mohawks that later came to be known as the Mohawk

Institute. Now it seemed that these 'Christians' had sold the land they had got from the Indians, which to Forbidden Voice was the same as stealing it.

Forbidden Voice knew that many of her people believed the Christian missionaries had no right to try to make Indians change their own religion and way of worship. Didn't it say in the Bible, at the very beginning of Genesis, 'And God said, "Let us make man in Our own image, after Our likeness, and let them have dominion over the fish of the sea and over the fowl of the air". So God created men in His own image, in the image of God created He him male and female created He them'?

And wasn't it only later, in Chapter Five of Genesis, that God created Adam and Eve to inhabit the Garden of Eden in the old world? Surely this meant that Adam and Eve were created to inhabit a specific place in the old world and that the Indians were the original man-beings created in the new world, with the eternal right to hunt and fish for their food?

Hadn't Christ told his apostles when he sent them to teach and baptize in the old world, 'I have other sheep which are not of this fold; them I will gather in'? Surely this meant the Indians were Christ's special charges, and that all the popes and kings and bishops of the old world had no authority to interfere.

Forbidden Voice had seen with her very own eyes evidence that the Creator kept an eye on his special children. A tornado had swept through one summer causing death and destruction in its path. When it had started to get very dark on the reserve, and they could see the funnel-shaped cloud coming from the west, all the families had been called together. As they watched, the funnel cloud lifted high aloft and passed over their heads. When it had gone past Indian territory, they could see it come to earth again and go on its angry way. Didn't this mean the Creator was not displeased with the red men?

Her mother had taught her a prayer in Mohawk to repeat every night before she went

to bed. All it said was 'God the Father, God the Son, God the Holy Ghost; Creator of the sun, the moon, the stars and the earth. Amen.' Its form was Christian, but she thought about it now and its spirit seemed to her more like a true Mohawk prayer. It was like the six annual festivals held at the other longhouses on the reserve. (The Mohawks were supposed to be Christians so their own longhouse had been destroyed.) The festivals were held according to the moon and their purpose was to thank the Creator for the seasons and for the ripening of each crop as it came on. This was her people's ancient religion, and it began to seem to her the purest way of worship, Wasn't it better than always asking the Creator to do something or to give something more than He already had?

Yet, even though the Indians worshipped the Creator in constant gratitude and remembrance, and were His charges, and practiced the stern morality of Handsome Lake, the white men called them heathens.

There was another thing. Forbidden Voice could read very well now, and one day among the Six Nations' records she came across a document. It was a letter containing a list and a speech. It seemed there had been a pledge to the Iroquois just before the American War of Independence that any of the Iroquois who remained loyal to England in her war would at the close of the war receive the protection of Britain. When the war was over, it had been required of her forefathers to prove in any way they could that they had fought for England's cause, and this is what they had sent.

January 3, 1782

May it please your Excellency:
I send herewith to your Excellency under the care of James Boyd, eight pecks of scalps, cured, dried, hooped and painted with all the Indian triumphal marks of which the following is invoice and explanation.

No. 1–Containing 43 scalps of Congress soldiers killed in different skirmishes. These are stretched on black hoops, four-inch diameter, the inside of the skin, painted red with a small black spot to note their being killed with bullets. Also, 62 of farmers, killed in their homes, the hoops red, the skin painted brown and marked with a hoe, a black circle all around to denote their being surprised in the night and a black hatchet in the middle signifying their being killed with that weapon.

No. 2–Containing 98 of farmers, killed in their homes, hoops red, figure of a hoe to mark their profession, great white circle and sun to show they were surprised in the daytime, a little red foot to show they stood upon their defence and died fighting for their lives and families.

No. 3–Containing 97 of farmers, hoops green to show they were killed in their fields, a large white circle with a little round mark on it for the sun to show that it was in the daytime, black bullet marks on some, hatchets on others.

No. 4–Containing 102 of farmers, mixed of the several marks above, only 18 marked with a little yellow flame to denote their being of prisoners burned alive after being scalped, their nails pulled out by the roots and other torments, one of these latter supposed to be of a rebel clergyman, his band being fixed to the hoop of his scalp. Most of the farmers appear by the hair to have been young or middle-aged men, there being but 67 very gray heads among them, which makes the service more essential.

No. 5–Containing 88 scalps of women, hair long, braided in the Indian fashion to show they were mothers, hoops blue, skin yellow ground with little red tadpoles to represent by way of triumph, the tears of grief occasioned to their relations, a black scalping knife or hatchet at the bottom to mark their being killed, with these instruments; 17 others hair very gray, black hoops, plain brown color, no mark but the short club to show they were knocked down dead or had their brains beat out.

No. 6–Containing 103 boys' scalps of various ages, small green hoops, whitish ground on the skin, red tears in the middle and

black bullet mark, knife, hatchet or club as their deaths happened.

No. 7–211 girls' scalps, big and little, small yellow hoops, white ground, tears, hatchet, club, scalping knife, etc.

No. 8 – This package is a mixture of all the varieties above mentioned to the number of 122 with a box of birch-bark containing 29 little infants' scalps of various sizes, small white hoops.

With these packs, the chiefs send to your Excellency the following speech:

Your Excellency's most obedient and humble servant,

Signed
James Crawford.

Speech

'Father, we send you herewith many scalps that you may see that we are not idle friends.

'Father, we wish to send these scalps over the water to the Great King that he may regard them and be refreshed and that he may see our faithfulness in destroying his enemies and be convinced that his presents have not been made to ungrateful people.

'Father, attend to what I am now going to say, it is a matter of much weight. The Great King's enemies are many and they grow fast in numbers. They were formerly like young panthers, they could neither bite nor scratch. We could play with them safely, we feared nothing they could do to us but now their bodies are become as big as the elk and strong as the buffalo. They also have got great and sharp claws, they have driven us out of our country by taking part in your quarrel. We expect the Great King will give us another country that our children may live after us and be his friends and children as we are. Say this for me to the Great King.

'Father, we have only to say further that your traders exact more than ever for their goods and our hunting is lessened by the war, so that we have fewer skins to give them. This ruins us. Think of some remedy.

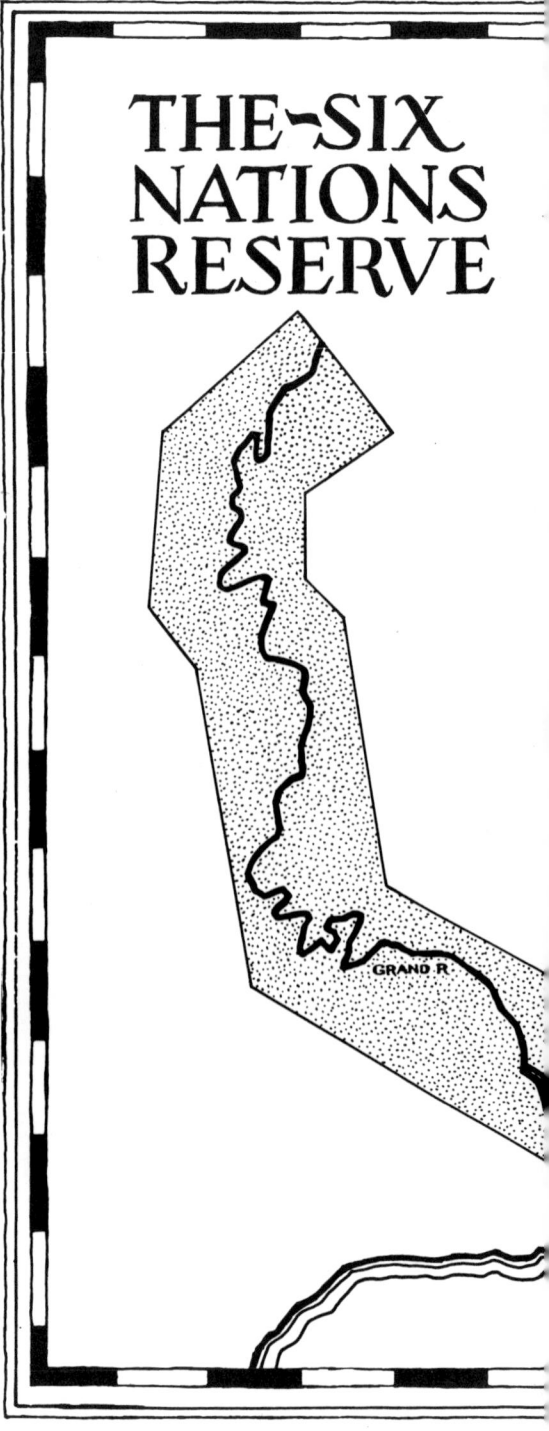

THE SIX NATIONS RESERVE

GRAND R.

LAKE ONTARIO

LAKE ERIE

'We are poor and you have plenty of every-thing. We know you will send us powder and guns and knives and hatchets, but we also want shirts and blankets. I do not doubt that your Excellency will think it proper to give some further encouragement to those honest people. The high prices they complain of are the necessary effect of the war. Whatever pre-sents may be sent for them through my hands shall be distributed with prudence and fidelity.

'I have the honour of being
Your Excellency's most obedient and most
humble servant.
James Crawford'

It was after sending this proof that the Six Nations had been given the lands in the Grand River Valley and had moved there from the United States and had rekindled their Great Council Fire in their new home. But the treaty of pledge, which had been executed on April 7, 1779, had promised the Six Nations not just land to replace what they had lost but the same status as before the war, which meant the right to be an independent nation; to be allies of the English, not British subjects; to be brothers of the sovereign with their own equal sovereignty.

And now what had happened? Their lands had been sold or stolen; the Canadian govern-ment treated them as silly children for whom it was quite all right to make laws without con-sultation; and the white men called them heathens.

Now there were even mutterings among some on the reserve that the Six Nations should abandon the ancient hereditary council of chieftains and have a white man's kind of elected government.

Forbidden Voice wondered what it would have been like for the Mohawks if there had never been a Captain Joseph Brant, though everyone seemed to think of him as an illustri-ous warrior and remembered him for saying in the English court, 'I bend my knee for no man.' For Brant, who was not even a chief but just a Mohawk warrior, was the one who had

127

JOSEPH BRANT

got the Six Nations mixed up with the white man and who had helped talk the Six Nations into fighting for England. And he was the one who had been so eager to see the Mohawks become Christians that he had destroyed their longhouse.

Though Forbidden Voice's father no longer went to the Christian church, the rest of the family did, and it was their strong custom at Easter to come back from wherever they might be to go to their own church.

This was why Forbidden Voice's sister came home from Brantford that Easter. She had come with her cousin and when her mother asked her why her husband did not come, she did not answer right away.

But after they had come back from the service and had dinner, the sister told her parents that her husband had been staying out almost every night all winter. She had found out from the place where he worked that he had been seeing a married woman. She had not talked to him about this because he never wanted to talk when he came home.

He had been out all the night before and had come in only as she was getting ready to leave for the trip to her parents' home. She had asked him to come with her to church, but he got very angry and said the devil himself could not make him go to church.

She returned to Brantford the same night. Afterwards Forbidden Voice was told that just as her sister reached home, a policeman stopped her and told her that if she wanted to see her husband alive she must go at once to the hospital. She had no money left to take a cab, so she walked. When she got there, they let her go in at once to see her husband. She hardly recognized him, his face was so disfigured. The doctor said he was dying, but he did not tell her what had happened. No one told her. They just gave her his blood-soaked suit to take home. She walked back all the way from the hospital, carrying the suit, and by the time she reached home she herself was soaked with his blood.

Her husband died that night. Afterwards another policeman told her that while she was gone for Easter, her husband and his brother had got into an argument over a girl. They were both big men and under the influence of liquor, and the older brother had thrown her husband down and jumped on his face and head and that was how he had died.

His body was released to a local undertaker directly from the hospital. But after the funeral the pallbearers, who were friends of his, began to wonder. The husband had been a tall man, while the coffin they had been given to carry was short and light.

Finally the widow and the man's father got an order to have the grave dug up. With some friends they went that night carrying lanterns, spades and shovels. They started to dig. All was silent but the noise of the shovels. When the coffin was opened the widow and the father moved closer. There was a gasp. The body in the coffin had no shroud to cover it. And it had no head. No one else could identify it, so the widow said her husband had had a birthmark on his chest that she would recognize. They let her look. Hardly above a whisper she said it was the body of her husband.

The white man's world was beginning to intrude on Forbidden Voice's life. Some of it, like what had happened to her sister's husband, made no sense to her at all.

WITCHCRAFT

Spells and remedies
Charms, exorcisms, medicine men
True stories and old
men's tales

In the May of one year, Forbidden Voice's father got pneumonia. She was older now, and one day while he was ill she was left alone in the house to nurse him. Suddenly she heard a great racket of trampling hoofs and splintering wood in the barn.

Forbidden Voice ran to look, and there were a neighbor's milking cows that had got loose and strayed into the barn, where they had already smashed the shafts of the democrat. Too worried about her father to be patient, she simply locked them in the barn. They bawled all night, their udders swollen with milk, and the next morning their owner found them and took them home. He was very angry.

Not that day but the next one, Forbidden Voice woke with a cramp in her leg. She tried to jump out of bed but she couldn't, and she found that both her legs were drawn up and wouldn't straighten out.

Her parents got doctors to look at her, but they could find nothing wrong. All the same, she couldn't walk. Her father, who was out of

bed by now, tried putting weights on her feet to straighten her legs, but that didn't work. All through the summer and early fall Forbidden Voice lay in bed paralyzed.

One night in late October a man came to the house who was a relative of the neighbor with the cows. He said he had come to see Forbidden Voice, and when they were alone he told her that the neighbor thought she had suffered long enough so he would prepare a medicine which he, the relative, would bring her. Forbidden Voice said she had no money to pay for medicine so the relative asked her whether she remembered locking the neighbor's cows in the barn. He said the neighbor would give her the medicine for nothing.

That same evening the relative returned. He gave Forbidden Voice a glass containing a dark transparent liquid that looked something like strong tea. He told her to take a glass of the liquid before bed, before she ate, any time she woke in the night, or any time the pain was severe. She took the first glass that very

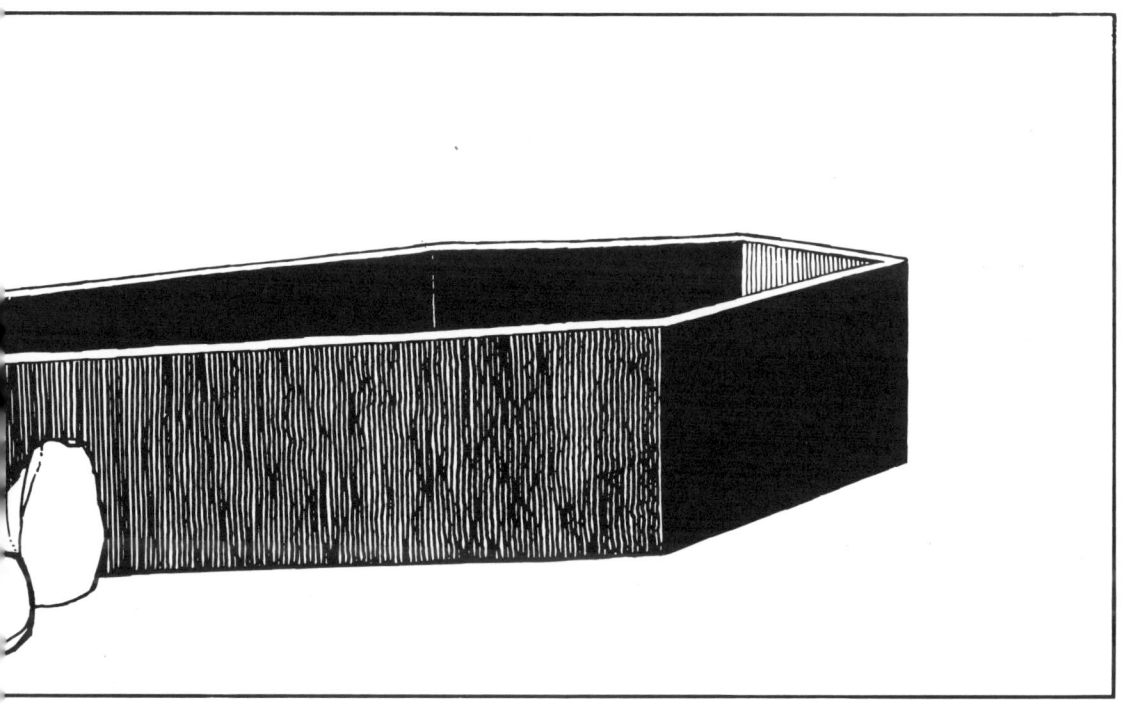

night and it was like water, with no taste. The next morning Forbidden Voice thought she felt different, though she was not sure how or why.

The third morning she was alone at breakfast. Her bed had been moved downstairs and into the kitchen, and this time when she wanted coffee she moved without thinking to get it for herself. She shoved herself upright, put her legs over the side and, leaning on a chair, pushed it to the stove to get the coffee pot. All at once she began to call and shout, 'I can walk.' As the family came running she put aside the chair and walked without it.

Until the visit from the neighbor's relative, Forbidden Voice had not thought she had anything but a natural sickness. But the idea that it was something else did not surprise her.

Witchcraft had been introduced originally among the Six Nations of Grand River by the Algonquins. Now there were believed to be witches and witch-men in every tribe on the reserve. It was said that when your house was

attacked by witchcraft you would be fore-warned. You would hear queer noises in the house – groaning and footsteps or knocking at the door when no one was there. Doors would open and close at will. It was also said that if a suspected witch approached your house, you should quickly place a chair for her and throw a handful of treated salt underneath it. If she were a real witch, she would refuse to sit on that chair and go to another instead.

Forbidden Voice was almost sure that she knew a witch. This was an old woman who lived alone, and in her kitchen she kept a little black pot with dried blood in it, which was supposed to be the blood of her victims.

Forbidden Voice was quite sure she also knew a witch-man. He lived nearby, and had the only pair of brown corduroy pants in the neighborhood, and he sometimes came to the farmhouse in the evening with the other men to gossip and tell stories. He had children who were playmates of her's, and once when they were playing at his place they got into his

133

possessions and found a crystal ball, and a tiny coffin and a tiny doll that would just fit into the coffin. Forbidden Voice knew what these were for: you stuck pins into the doll, or else you put the doll into the coffin and put the coffin in the ground. She and her playmates scared each other by making up their own spells to use with the doll and the coffin.

One night she and an older relative were coming home from a party around midnight, and just when they got within sight of their own house, they saw a tongue of flame in the dirt road in front of them. It was about ten feet away and it burned up from the road to a height of about three feet.

As they stared at it they saw a hand guiding the flame—it was an open palm which guided the flame higher or lower as it commanded.

When the flame lowered they could see distinctly, in its light, a man's legs clad in brown corduroy pants. Corduroy Pants seemed unaware or unconcerned that anyone was so close, as though he were doing something he had to do regardless of who saw him. Forbidden Voice stayed watching, fascinated, but her relative ran to the farmhouse for help; and as she ran Corduroy Pants moved off down the road with the flame ahead of him, guiding it up and down with the palm of his hand.

Her brother came out of the house and walked a long way down the road, but he saw no sign of Corduroy Pants or of any flame. The next day Forbidden Voice and her relative went along the road again, but there was no sign or mark on the road where the flame had been.

There were many ways of making people sick or of killing them. Children were often attacked in order to punish parents. The child would develop a high temperature and complain of a bear lurking in the room. Sometimes the fever and terror would lead to convulsions, and the only remedy for this was to contact the Bear Society.

Forbidden Voice herself remembered vaguely, like a terrible nightmare, a time when as a tiny child she was ill; and every time she awoke

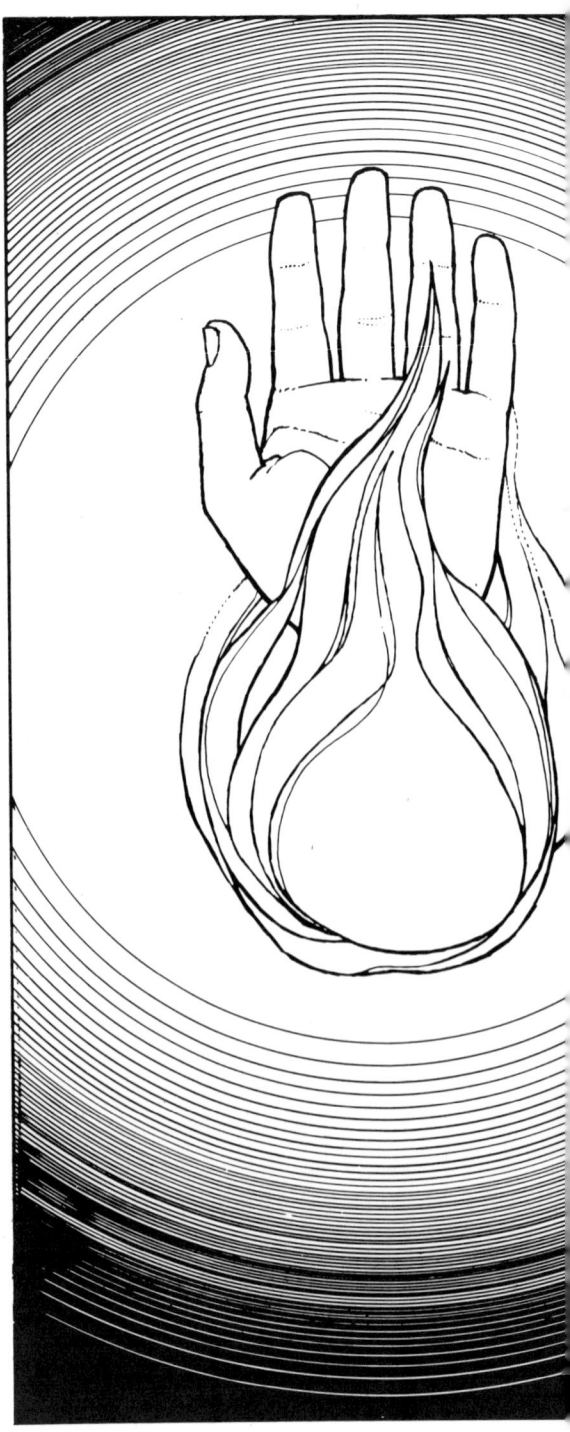

there was a bear lurking in the shadows and she screamed and screamed, Then people came and made a feast and ate nuts and drank berry water while they performed a lengthy ceremony, and afterwards Forbidden Voice was cured.

Sometimes a child would become ill after someone had given her a new corn-husk doll. She would refuse food and get very weak, and at night she would seem to be afraid of something, and would toss around in bed restlessly. Usually the parents got their fortune read to find out the cause of the child's illness, and it would turn out that the person who made the corn-husk doll had been evil and did not have pure, wholesome thoughts. The parents would prepare a purification ceremony and invite the people who understood the ceremony. During it the doll would be destroyed and another made to take its place.

There were other ways of antagonizing a person. An ill-wisher could throw dirt from a cemetery in the path of his victim and according to the wish, cripple the person or do him other sorts of harm. Or he could make a doll, then prepare a concoction of roots and herbs, dip a new sewing needle into the concoction and then stick the doll wherever he wanted to cause pain. If it were in the leg, the person concerned might become a cripple.

In many cases telepathy was used. An object like a pin or a needle would be saturated in witch potion, then stuck into the body of the victim by the supernatural powers of the evil one. The bewitched would become very ill at that instant. The most evil witches work their spells with the help of the devil, whose name is O-nes-sonh-ro-noh.

Then there were the luck charms, which could be used for good or evil.

Many Indian families own a luck charm. Once they have one, it stays in the family forever and is passed down from each generation to the next. The oldest surviving member automatically becomes the owner and master of the charm. It is wrong to use the charm to harm others, but an evil owner will do so.

135

The luck charm could be the carving of a certain kind of black bug that lives on animal or human sinews. Commanded by an evil person, the bugs would attack the sinews of an intended victim. If the owner neglected the luck charm, or forgot to give it the feast that was his annual hire, the bug would attack the owner and his family. It is well to stay on the good side of your luck charm.

The luck charm could be a skeleton, who could be set to feast upon the victim, so that the victim becomes thinner and thinner and finally dies. The doctors might say that the person died of cancer, or tuberculosis.

The luck charm could be a corn-husk doll. Or it could be an animal or a bird. The victim would be disturbed night after night by the screech of an owl or the roar of a lion until he was a wreck of himself.

There is an annual ceremony at a certain time of year when witch spirits are expelled from the neighborhood. At other times the only people who can fight witchcraft are the medicine men and medicine women. They have studied the witch charms and can offset the devil action. For example, they know how to extract a bewitched needle from the victim's body; they can even turn the bewitched object back on the person who sent it.

But the sincere medicine man does not indulge in evil practices. He does not sell compelling charms to be used as love potions. He does not set a price for the fortunes he tells with roots but takes what is willingly offered. He does not burn the sacred tobacco to confuse the minds of his enemies or to guide luck charms on evil missions. The burning of the tobacco is a sacred mission for him. The sacred tobacco is instrumental in correcting all evil mishaps.

The medicine man's powers are akin to the witch's, but the medicine man calls on the Creator for his powers, and seeks to do good. The witch calls on the devil, who is called O-nes-sonh-ro-noh.

Among the Grand River Indians there are many true stories and old men's tales about witches and luck charms.

A witch light

This happened in Forbidden Voice's lifetime, near where she lived.

There was a vacant house near the edge of a forest on the Six Nations Reserve, and people said they often saw a light there, as big and round as a rubber ball. The light would bounce on the roof, on the window and on the door and seemed to be everywhere.

One night some people saw this light from a house nearby. A woman among them offered to go and investigate if someone would lead her over the rough ground so that she need not take her eyes off the light. Her husband said he would go and led her through the field as she watched it. The light kept bouncing up and down on the roof and then from the roof to the window and to the doorknob and back on to the roof again. When they were about three feet from the house the light suddenly disappeared.

They looked through the window of the main building, which had no blinds. They could see nothing. They went around to the back and looked through the kitchen window. The ball of light was there on the south wall, quivering as though it sensed their presence. As they watched, it bounced up and down and then split into five small flames like candle lights. The five flames stayed in that state for a few seconds before they began to quiver harder and harder until they fused into a ball of light again.

The woman and her husband were baffled. The man led the woman back towards the fields, walking backwards so they could keep their eyes on the house. They had only gone ten feet when they saw the light back on the roof.

This light was seen again when on another night a woman was returning to her house late. She saw the light bounce off the roof of the vacant house and go bouncing along to her own house where it sat on her clothesline for a few seconds. Then it bounced up and down the length of her line. When she reached her own doorstep, the light was back at the vacant house near the edge of the forest.

The lady who owned the house was old and sick in the hospital. The woman decided to go and see her and tell her about the light. After she told her, the old lady smiled and said it was on account of all the medicine she had in that house.

The old lady told her not to be afraid, because the light would never hurt her. Shortly after that, the old lady died. The vacant house burned to the ground and the light was never seen again.

The fox
This is a story an old man told.

A little girl had lost her mother and father, who had gone into the dense forest in search of food and never returned. They were later found by neighbors – they had been attacked by some wild animal. After the funeral, an old lady offered to take care of the little girl, who was only four. She told the child she was her grandmother and would always love her as her own.

This old lady was a witch who lived alone and was very glad to have an heiress to her profession. She knew the ancient tradition that all witchcraft must be handed down through blood descent or adoption. She had a 'box of tricks' which she kept on the shelf. In this box were hides and skins of various animals, and feathers of birds, a piece of a skull, a doll made from a corn husk, a miniature coffin, and roots and herbs.

It was required of her by the master of all evil to keep using these tricks or they would turn on her and kill her. Thus was she compelled to torment and to destroy.

One night at midnight the little girl heard queer noises in the house. She got out of bed and looked through the keyhole of her bedroom door, and she saw her grandmother with her box of tricks performing a ceremony and mumbling words she could not understand. Finally the grandmother put a root into her mouth, threw a hide over her back, turned into an animal, and ran out of the house.

The little girl went back to sleep, and in the morning her grandmother was back in her own bed. Every night at midnight the child watched

140

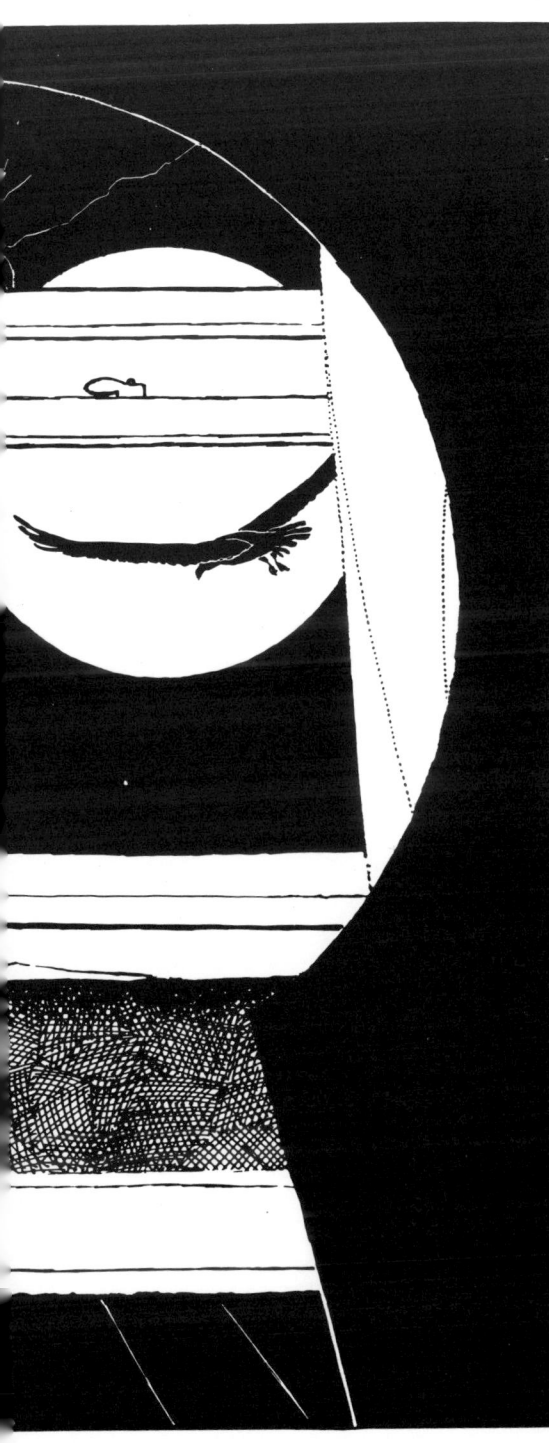

the same procedure. Sometimes the old lady would put a feather of a bird on her back and would turn into a bird and fly away. The old lady did not know her granddaughter had seen anything.

One night the witch was away, the little girl got into her box of tricks. She copied exactly what she had seen her grandmother do so often. When she threw a skin over her back she turned into a silver fox and started running all over the house. The old witch sensed something had happened and hurried home. As she approached the house she heard noises of scratching and running. She jerked the door open. A beautiful silver fox ran out into the forest.

It was many, many nights the old lady looked for the silver fox, but she never saw her granddaughter again. Now she knew she had to look for somebody else to carry on or she would be destroyed, for already a skull was on her doorstep each night as she returned home.

The black dog

An old man who lived alone in a small house was sick.

He had a daughter and a son, who had homes of their own, but the daughter came and sat by his bedside night after night for she was in awe of him. But after a time the daughter wanted to go back and rest at her own home for one night. Neighbors promised to look after her father so she could get some sleep, and she asked her brother to walk home with her.

On their way, just before they reached the cross-roads, she said to her brother, 'What would do if you were walking and talking to a dog instead of me?' Her brother answered, 'I have heard rumours about your witchcraft, which I never believed, but if they are true I believe I would kill you.'

His sister gave a loud weird laugh and he turned to look at her. To his surprise he saw a small black dog running and jumping beside him. He started to kick at the dog. It jumped over an old rail fence, so he went after it. But his boot kept missing. He was cross and almost out of breath when he heard his sister laughing. He turned around and she was back on the road in her natural form.

He was angry and did not want to walk with her any farther. He reminded her about the rumors that she had killed her own husband. He reminded her that some day she would be on her own deathbed and then her magical powers could not save her from death.

It was just getting daylight when they reached her home. The brother made a fire in her stove and she prepared breakfast. When everything was ready they sat at the table to eat.

They were both silent. The brother was thinking that the only person who could reason with his sister was their father, but he was now so ill that he could not talk any more. Suddenly they heard a noise that seemed to come from under the table. They looked at one another, and the sister pointed under the table and screamed. Her brother stood up and looked too.

There before their eyes were their father's legs and feet; they could see as far as his knees.

The brother said they should hurry back to their father for what they saw could be a sign that he needed them. They went at once, and hardly had they stepped inside his house than their father died. The brother and sister agreed not to tell anyone what else had happened that day.

After the funeral was over, the sister returned to her home, called a meeting of the Witchcraft Society and related the strange episode to them. The oldest member of the society told her she was caught between two minds – inclined to listen to her brother and forsake witchcraft, and inclined to carry on. The only way to clear her conscience was to decide now one way or the other. She decided to carry on: after all her father, whom she had feared, was dead.

People were beginning to be afraid of her and avoid her. They gave her what she asked of them, for whenever anyone refused she became very ill. She piled up ill-gotten riches and gloated over her power, which was no longer a secret.

After a time the neighbors did not see her going about any more. Nobody volunteered to go to her house, but someone told her brother of her disappearance. Reluctantly he went to her house where he found her very ill in bed. She would not allow him to call a doctor but asked him just to stay with her for her time was near to the end. One of the neighbors came in to sit with him, and together they watched while she re-lived the days of her life, screaming to the top of her voice.

The sister died in the early hours of a beautiful day. Just as she died the watchers heard a loud rumble. The door flew open and two great pigs burst into the room and went to her bed. After she was buried, her home became so haunted it had to be destroyed.

Her brother remembered what he told her, that some day she would be dying and her magical powers could not save her from death.

The owl

This is a story Forbidden Voice's own mother told her; she knew the people it had happened to.

A man and his sister were always at odds. She was jealous of his great ambition and delighted in devising ways to trick him and to hurt him in his business. Being a woman, she had no strength to cause him bodily harm. But she had heard there was a Witchcraft Society where they could teach her to become a bird or an animal and to contact people without making herself known. She thought if this were true it would serve her ends and she would join them. So she went to the home of an old man who was a member of the society.

She left her house at midnight, in the dark and cold, and it was almost morning when she reached his home. Groping her way in the dark, she found his laneway. She was startled to see him sitting on top of his gatepost. He said, 'Here you are at last. I have been expecting you.' Together they went into his house, and the woman told him of her decision to join their society. She wanted to know what she had to do to become eligible. He warned her it would not be easy, but if she were in earnest

and her decision final, he would consult his colleagues and would know by the next night. He would expect her to be at his home at the same time.

The next night she reached his home at the same time and found him sitting on the gatepost. 'Come', he said, 'we do not have much time. The society has accepted you and I shall take you there right now for your first lesson.'

The meeting place of the Witchcraft Society was the center of a dense forest. Just before they reached this place, the old man gave her a root to put in her mouth and told her to bathe her eyelids with saliva. She did as she was told. Then he told her to look and tell him what she saw. To her amazement she saw not people but animals and birds sitting on old dead logs near a swamp. She could not tell who they were in human form, and they were calling her to come and join them. She turned to speak to the old man, but in his place there was a roaring lion.

The society was well organized. They had a speaker who spoke to her in his natural voice, giving her instructions and telling her she could not back out of her bargain now. He told her she would have to sacrifice the person she loved the most to be her first victim–this was the price for becoming a full-fledged witch. After that the woman could choose her own victim, but she had to destroy one life annually in order to have control over the evil powers. Only then would she be able to torment and make people ill.

This was the reason why the woman had wanted to join the Witchcraft Society, and if she had to sacrifice a loved one to be able to do these things, she would. And she did.

She had to keep human blood in a black iron pot the society gave her. Soon she was able to transform herself into anything which suited her purpose. The thing she liked most to be was an owl, and she would pick out her victim and go at night to sit on a tree close to the house.

Her brother had a fine-looking horse that he prized very highly. He gave it special care and kept it in its own little barn. Every night before he went to bed, he would go to the barn to see that the horse was comfortable. Dealers often came and offered high prices for the horse, but he always refused to part with it.

One night after he had gone to bed he was awakened by a harsh noise. It sounded like an owl screeching close by, and then again it sounded like someone talking. Persuading himself he had imagined it, he went back to sleep.

The same thing happened night after night. Then one night he heard a commotion in the barn, and he ran to it and found his horse wild with fright. An owl which was perched on the barn roof flew away just then, cackling shrilly.

Now he was worried. Early the next morning he consulted a medicine man who was his friend. Though he was only a medicine man to doctor people, he might be able to give counsel.

The brother told the medicine man all that had happened, and the medicine man said it was the work of a witch. He told the brother to put silver in his rifle bullets, and when the owl came again to shoot at it. He would not need to take careful aim for the silver bullet would find its own mark.

That night he was ready and waiting for the owl, and when he heard a commotion in the barn he took his gun and ran out. The owl was in the tree again and seemed to hoot with glee.

He shot at it and brought it to the ground. Then he ran into the barn to see his horse. It stood there drenched in blood, for the owl had cut an artery and the horse was bleeding to death.

The brother came out. He was sure the owl would be there on the ground, but it was gone. He ran back to the house, lit a lantern and returned to the spot where it had fallen. All he saw were traces of blood.

He tracked the trail of drops of blood which led straight to his sister's house, and walked right in without knocking. Her husband was there and told him that his wife had had an accident and that he was on his way to get a doctor. She was bleeding very badly.

The doctor came and questioned her about how she had got a bullet in her side, but she refused to answer. Just before she died she transferred her membership in the Witchcraft Society to another member of her family, for the little black pot with the human blood is passed on from one generation to another. If the pot is not kept replenished, the family soon becomes extinct.

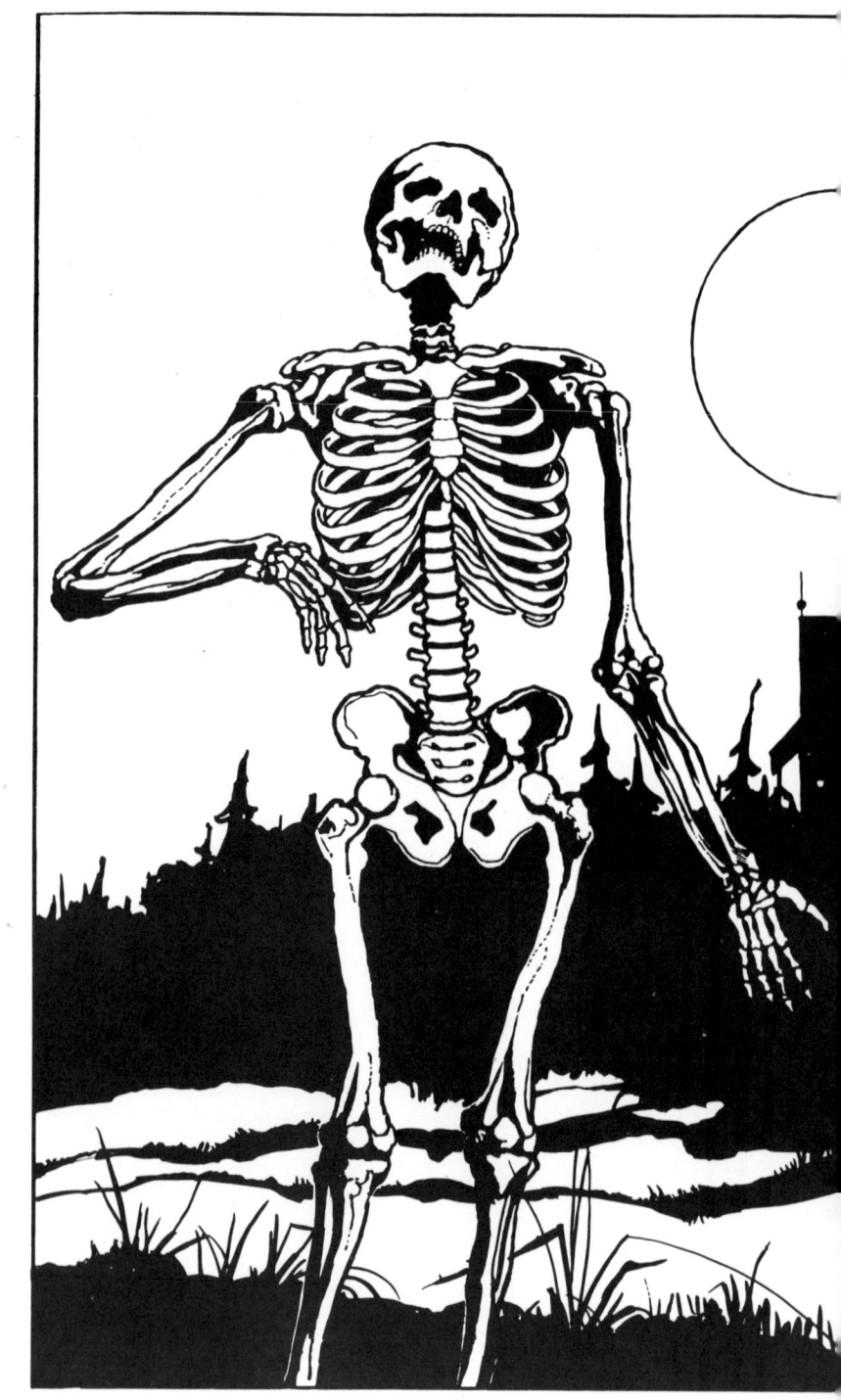

THE
SKELETON
LUCK-CHARM

This is how the family of Forbidden Voice came to get its own luck charm.

Her father fell ill again, this time very seriously. The family sent for a white doctor, who examined him, but left without saying anything or leaving any medicine. Forbidden Voice nursed her father as best she could, but one day when she had left him for a while she returned to find him by turns fainting and delirious, mumbling things that made no sense. Gathering together her courage, she went in to town to see the doctor herself, but he said he could see no sign of serious illness and that her father was healthy and strong and would be all right. The doctor did promise to pay another visit in a few days, but the family waited in vain; he never came.

Meanwhile her father had fallen into a coma and was getting sicker and sicker. When the daughter went to the doctor's office again, she was told he had gone on vacation.

As a pine tree chief in the confederacy, her father was a popular and respected man, and the word of his illness soon spread. One night ten medicine men from the tribes came to the house. She let them in and showed them to her father's bedroom. Then, while she sat trembling and holding his limp hand, they performed a lengthy ceremony. She couldn't see much of it, for they had turned the lamp low and were crouched in a circle in one corner of the bedroom around a little black iron pot where roots were brewing. But lights like fire-flies sparked here and there, and the sounds of wild animals filled the room.

Then the medicine men called her. They said that she was her father's daughter and must take part in the ceremony. Full of fear she crouched with them over the pot and saw that they were passing to each in turn two objects that they clapped together, creating a spark that flew out to fall into the pot.

Then it was her turn. She was handed the objects, which seemed to be two round stones one for each hand. But as she raised them to clap them together in imitation, the stones wrenched themselves violently from her hands and flew to the corners of the room. A rush of

noise filled the room. The little black pot shattered.

The medicine men retreated and conferred gravely among themselves.

Finally they came to her. It was too late to help her father. He would die by the wicked magic of a witch and they could not save him. But they could do something for those left behind. They would prepare a potion in a small bowl, and in the bowl would appear the person who was guilty of the illness, and the family would recognize her face. Then the medicine men would give the family a protector.

They all went downstairs now to the rest of the family, and there the medicine men told the family to face the wall and not to try to see what they were doing. All the lights were put out, and in the total darkness Forbidden Voice listened as they took the lid off the stove. She smelled the sacred tobacco burning. She heard them calling loudly to the dead, while they shuffled to the tom-tom beat, and bones rattled in rhythm, and the incense of the tobacco filled the room.

When the ceremony was done, the medicine men withdrew to the woods beyond, and there they performed another ceremony. Then they left.

After a time they returned to the house and brought a skeleton with them. Forbidden Voice knew that it would be the skeleton of an Indian who had died with the ancient beliefs – for this was necessary – and that it would have been taken from the Indian burial ground on the reserve.

The medicine men buried the skeleton in the pathway beside the house and instructed it to protect the family from harm and to be obedient if it was given a mission to do. They told the family to feed the skeleton once a year by making a feast for the dead.

And so Forbidden Voice's father died.

The skeleton remained as the family's luck charm. They could send him on missions to avenge their wrongs. They could burn the sacred tobacco and instruct him to cripple people they wished to harm or to feast on their enemies till they died. (The doctors would say it was cancer.) But Forbidden Voice's family believed these practices were wrong and didn't try them.

The skeleton could also be sent to chase pests or ill-wishers as far as the next concession road, sometimes frightening them so much that they would have had to seek shelter in someone's home until morning when they were brave enough to go on their way. If the skeleton chases you, the only way to shake him off is to eat half of whatever you have and throw the other portion on the ground for him.

All the family, and others too, have heard him cry out. The sound is high-pitched and piercing, like the sound of someone blowing into an empty bottle, or the sound of a live fly trapped in a jar and trying to get out. They hear him when someone dies, or if witchcraft attacks the house, or if he is getting restless.

When he gets restless it is time to make him a feast. That is his hire, and if they neglected it he might turn on them. It does not pay to get on the wrong side of the skeleton.

So one night they prepared a meal. It was an ordinary meal of potatoes, meat, rice, corn soup, corn bread—that is, the main course of a dead feast. The table was set and there was a ceremony. Then all the relatives sat down to partake of the meal, and the skeleton's portion was set aside on the old fall-leaf table. At the end of the meal there was a farewell ceremony to the dead, and the family gave its instructions to the skeleton.

The sacred tobacco was burned.

Then the lamp was turned down low to burn throughout the night and the skeleton's feast was left for him.

It is all right to clear away such a feast in the morning, but the food that is left, even the scraps of sugar, must be burned.

There is a saying that if you give any part of the dead feast food to a dog or a cat, he will die.

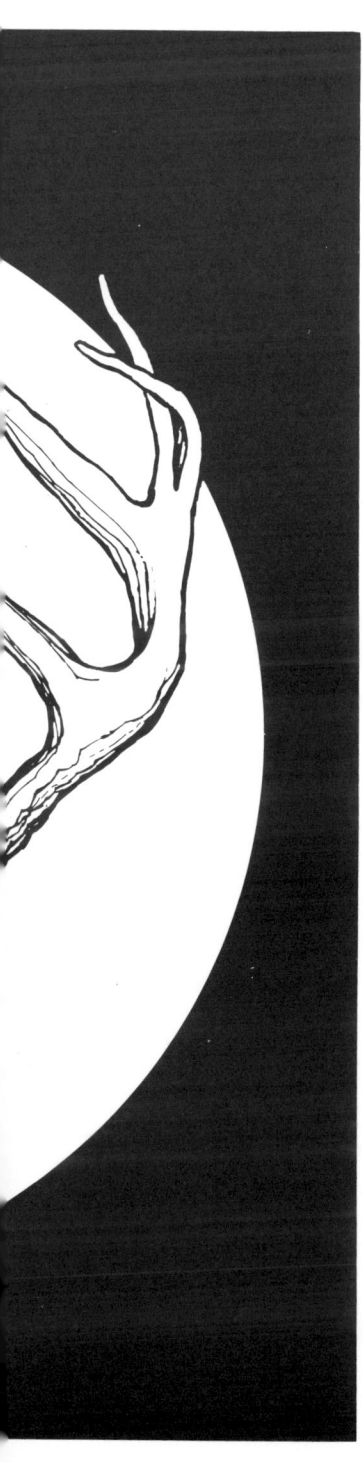

A NEW CLAN MOTHER

Forbidden Voice assumes her
destined role
History and records of the
Six Nations

Years before, Forbidden Voice had been taken by her mother to the ceremony of the hanging up of the horns of power. Her mother's old chief had been dying, and this had been the little girl's first Indian rite. Now the chief's successor was dead in his turn. Forbidden Voice's mother, the chief matron, was in bed, sick and hemorrhaging. There would be no one to take her part in the ceremony of the taking away of the horns.

Her mother summoned two of the nine Mohawk chiefs to her bedside and, in their presence, transferred her power to Forbidden Voice. Her big sister had been judged unfit, for now she had gone to live with the white people, but Forbidden Voice had kept herself pure.

She took the wampum beads and went with the chiefs, and there beside the coffin of the dead Mohawk lord performed the ceremony she remembered so well.

She was a princess, and now she was a clan mother and she was just eighteen.

The little Native girl, Forbidden Voice of the Six Nations, is now a grown woman, rich in memories of her happy childhood and in the stories and legends of her ancestors.

When they were still holding 'get togethers' at her home, these were no longer happy occasions, for the aged people who came were sad and spoke solemnly in whispers. Forbidden Voice knew something terrible was wrong and she vowed she would find out. She went in search of documents in the ancient homestead and found many valuable papers. The old people were huddled together and talked about the present events. The old Council of the Confederacy was cast aside by the Order-In-Council of the Canadian Government in 1924, and an elected council approved by the same government and set up in the heart of the capital of the Six Nations. Forbidden Voice remembered the dream of the old chief, about his pony with the two heads, how the native head welcomed the blond head and his tribe to find refuge and shelter with the red men and

how the blond head stretched his neck and wound it around the red man's head and killed him. Now the blond heads had made a law which was called the Indian Act to destroy the wonderful heritage of the natives who once rode the whole of the western hemisphere.

Forbidden Voice in her search for documents found many records. For example, in the month of May of 1710, five chiefs of the Six Nations had been sent to England as a delegation on tribal affairs. In England these chiefs were known as Indian Kings of the Six Nations. They were well received and created a great sensation not only in the capital but throughout the kingdom. After the reception of Her Majesty, they were taken to St James's in two coaches by Sir Charles Cotteral and were introduced again to the royal presence by the Duke of Shrewsbury, where they delivered a speech on the occasion.

At the beginning of the American War of Independence the people of the Six Nations became faithful allies of the British Crown under the leadership of Captain Joseph Brant. He had an illustrious career as warrior, statesman and diplomat and he practiced the principle of valor in warfare, tolerance and devotion to his native people and to the British Crown. He made many trips across the ocean to England to converse with the King about the welfare of the Indians.

During the American Revolution, General Washington sent an army under General Sullivan to punish the Iroquois for cruel and bloody work in behalf of their close alliance with Great Britain. There were over forty Iroquois villages totally destroyed. The League of the Six Nations was so badly disrupted that it was forced to find shelter in Canada under the protection of the British Government. The Great Council Fire of the Six Nations was re-kindled on the Grand River in Ontario, Canada, and the Council Fire is still burning. Portions of the Indian tribes which remained in New York State re-lighted a fire at Onondaga to re-establish the ancient form of their

153

government, but this was only partly success-
ful since the seat of government had forever
departed to the Grand River.

Forbidden Voice found other documents
which she treasured very much. One of them
was a treaty between the Six Nations and the
Twelve United Colonies of the United States;
another was a record of the General Council of
the Six Nations, held in June 1870, and the list
of delegates from the different bands of Indians
in western and eastern Canada.

She also found the speech of Magistrate
O. M. Martin, a native son of the Six Nations,
given at the opening of the National Folk
Festival in 1947; 'I am a Canadian. I have no
country, this is my country and it was my
people who were here when the white man
came and welcomed them as settlers among
us.'

The history of loyalty of the Six Nations
was unsurpassed. There were 292 warriors
who took part in the First World War, 23 of
whom were killed in action. The first to give
his life was Lieutenant Cameron D. Brant, a
great, great-grandson of the famous Captain
Joseph Brant.

The first Red Cross organization to be
formed on any Indian Reserve was the Women
of the Six Nations in October, 1914.

Lieutenant Colonel Morgan was the Superintendent of the Six Nations for twelve years
and gave his farewell address in 1935. He had
seen many changes take place. He was instrumental in the changing of the government from
that of the Council of Hereditary Chiefs to a
council elected by its people. It was his pro-
clamation in 1924 that announced the change
and the institution of the Royal Canadian
Mounted Police in Ohsweken on Grand River
Lands.

Colonel Morgan said he looked forward to
remaining with the elected council for another
three years by the extension of the Order-In-
Council, but politics must be served and the
superintendency is too desirable a political
plum to remain undisturbed when opportunity
and expediency call. In closing he said that his
memories of the Grand River would remain

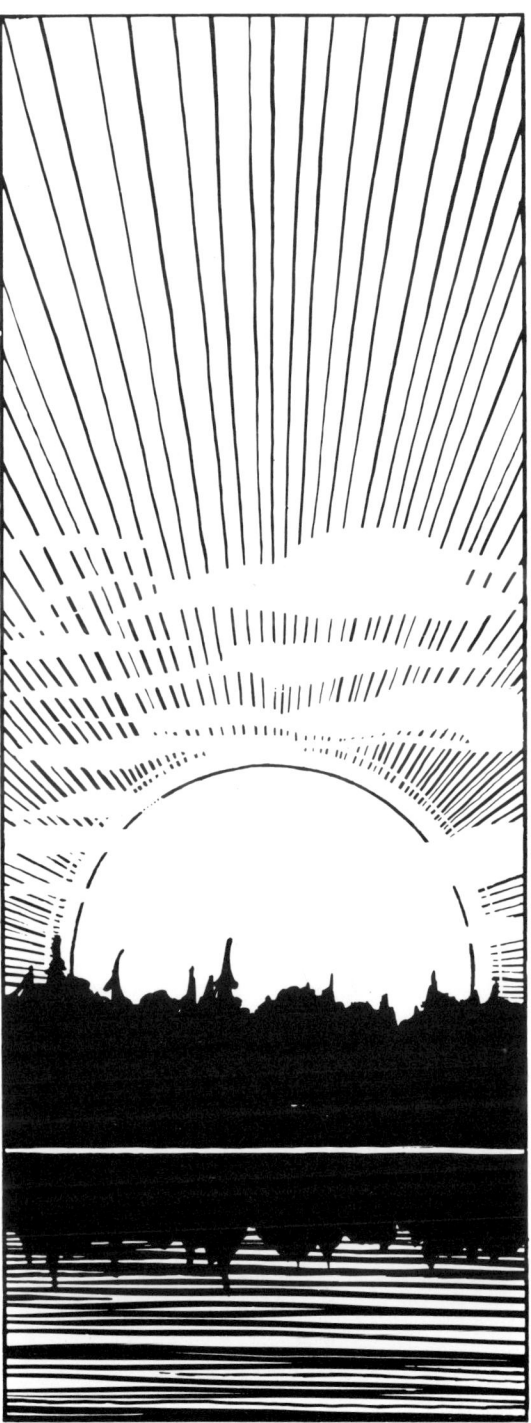

ever with him. In the words of Thomas Moore, he said, 'When time who steals our years away shall steal our pleasures too, the memory of the past will stay and half our joys renew.'

Major E. P. Randle another superintendent. of the Six Nations gave an interesting address to members of the Brantford Optimists Club:

'This country we call ours once belonged to the Indians, before us they enjoyed all its grandeur and beauty, before us they were sustained by the bounty of its earth, river and forest. That's all gone, none of us can possibly realize the pangs they feel when they realize the great heritage they have given and what a price they have paid. It's up to all of us to remember them for the generous hearted, gallant and courteous race they are today.

'In our cause and behalf the proud Indians of this district have sacrificed their freedom as individual nations. First while historians verify that the Indians' physical condition was near perfect and that they were of high morality and self-discipline.

'In every way they were found to be physically, spiritually and morally a high type of race.

'They had a religion that has been falsely described in their "longhouse" civilization. They worship the Great Spirit with six annual festivals occurring at various seasons.

'We do owe to the Six Nations unquestionably the fact that North America is ours for we could never have defeated the French without the Indians' assistance.'

I have had a long life, and I am a grandmother now, and these are memories and stories I have hoarded all that long time up till now.

But these are not all my stories or memories. Some things I know I would not tell to anyone, except perhaps my little granddaughter if she becomes clan mother in her turn. And I think some of the things I know I would not tell even to her.

I married the boy next door, for he was a Mohawk, of the Bear Clan, and I had in mind my vows. My husband was a shy, gentle, good man. He died twenty years ago.

I have lived on the reserve all these years, in a house about two miles from the lovely old farmhouse where I grew up. I have seen a lot of trouble in that time.

I have seen the old council of the confederacy cast aside by Order-In-Council of the Canadian Government in 1924, and an elected council, approved by the Canadian Government, set up in the heart of the capital of the Six Nations. I can tell you many of us do not recognize that elected council as our government.

I have seen my people cheated of still more of their land. The market-place in Brantford, which was the old Indian trading post where my mother and father sold their produce on Saturdays, has been turned into a parking lot.

I have seen my people working for white bosses, and so timid that they took all the pushing around and scolding that was handed out. That I never took, though I was punching a time-clock in Brantford till I was sixty.

I have worked for my people, and gone many times to Ottawa to fight for them. Sometimes I have thought that I could burn the sacred tobacco and send the skeleton luck charm to cripple my people's enemies or confuse their minds, but that I have never done.

I am, of course, a medicine woman, which is my gift from the Creator and is what seeing the tiny deer meant, just as the old chief told my mother. Only a few people in my tribe know I am one, and those few don't speak of it except in time of trouble. In time of trouble, even if it is at the far other end of the reserve, I know about it before nightfall. I heard the other day that a lot of people on the reserve are practising witchcraft these days – mostly young people who are restless, and would like to prove to the world that these arts of our forefathers have not been lost.

I still can't help looking into the tea-leaves and seeing the future, so these days when I make tea for myself I make it with tea-bags.

I still have dreams and look for meanings.

I dreamed once that I went to the door of a longhouse here on the reserve. It was not, of course, the Mohawk longhouse, thanks to Joseph Brant. But it was one of the others where the Indians hold their own ceremonies.

When I got there the door would not open. I tried again and again, but it seemed as though something was pushing against it, holding it closed.

So I went around to the side, to a window, and looked in. There was the faithkeeper, crouched in horror in a corner. And the rest of the longhouse was filled with a serpent, as big around as a seven-inch pipe, lying from one end of the room to the other.

That's one dream I think has already come true.